cowlgirls 2

cowlgirls2

the neck's favorite knits

cathy carron

161 Avenue of the Americas, New York, NY 10013
sixthandspringbooks.com

Editor
HOLLY RUCK

**Vice President/
Editorial Director**
TRISHA MALCOLM

Editorial Assistant
JACOB SEIFERT

Publisher
CAROLINE KILMER

Yarn Editor
MATTHEW SCHRANK

Creative Director
JOE VIOR

Executive Editor
CARLA SCOTT

Production Manager
DAVID JOINNIDES

Instructions Editor
MARI LYNN PATRICK

President
ART JOINNIDES

Instructions Assistant
CEVRI CIVELEK

Chairman
JAY STEIN

Technical Illustrations
LORETTA DACHMAN

Photography
JACK DEUTSCH

Stylist
JOANNA RADOW

Hair/Makeup
ELENA LYAKIR

Library of Congress Cataloging-in-Publication Data
is available from the Library of Congress.

Manufactured in China

1 3 5 7 9 10 8 6 4 2

First Edition

contents

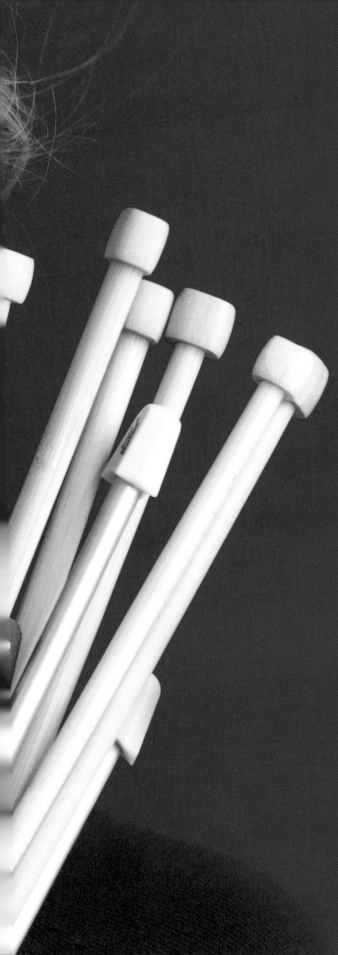

introduction

Welcome back cowl girls (and cowl boys)!

Because one collection of cowls could never be enough, here's a brand new group for you to try! This time around, there are new stitches, new shapes, and new configurations. For extra fun, I've included a few hats and some rogue dickey shapes and collars. There's something for every style!

Having myriad design options at your fingertips allows you to both test your knitting skills and create pieces that complement you and your wardrobe. In this collection, you'll find an exciting set of technical challenges that include:

• Inserting zippers either set within a seam or on top of knitted fabric

• Shifting yarn gauges within a pattern

• Piecing together motifs and then picking up and knitting a decorative edge around the assembled pieces

• Using multiple colors for Fair Isle, intarsia lettering, and mosaic work

• Incorporating paillettes, sequins, or pony beads

• Creating textured, decorative edgings and other stitchery such as drop-stitches, short rows, bobbles, ripples, and loops

Adding these technical options to your toolbox will enable you to create cowls best suited to your needs. And, best of all, you'll have the ability to express yourself artistically.

Before you choose a design, make sure to consider the shape of the cowl. A collarless coat with a rounded neck would look great with a ribbed dickey inserted inside the neck, a dickey with a sequin edge on the outside, or just about any neck covering. For an even more dramatic look, consider an oversized, wrapped cowl. Coats with large collars, however, often play by different rules. They might look good with a cowl that hugs the neck or is narrower with a wrap and drape down the front. Coats with small collars can work well with just about any cowl shape, depending on how it relates to the collar structure.

I hope you have fun perusing the entire collection as each design has a special feature or purpose for its creation. Choose your favorite shape, pick a design that screams your name, buy some gorgeous yarn, and get started!

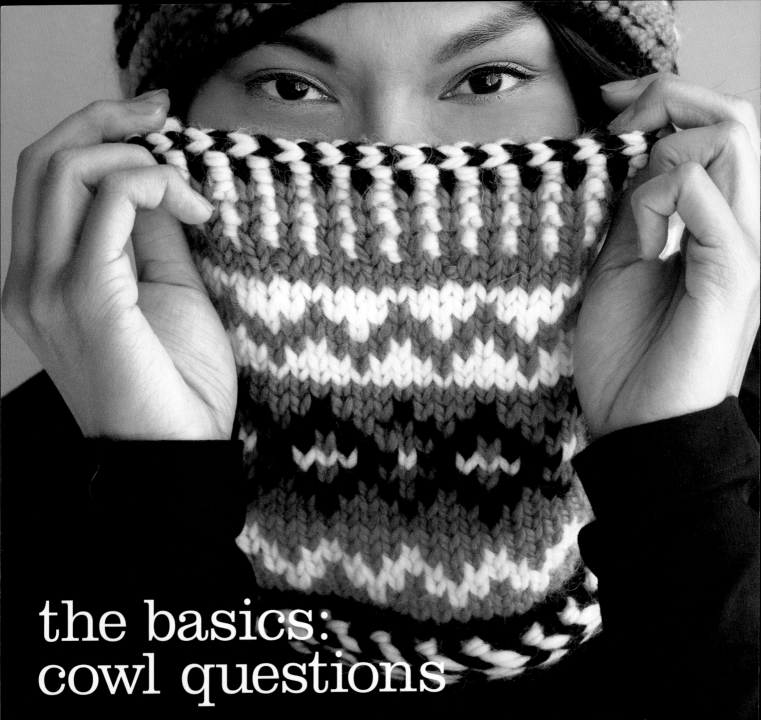

the basics:
cowl questions

Before we jump right into the patterns, you probably
have some questions:
What exactly is a cowl? A gaiter? And their
many permutations? How are cowls and gaiters
constructed? What kind of yarn is best for knitting
cowls? Read on for answers to these and other
burning questions!

In addition to classic cowls, this book features many

other shapes and designs for knitted neckwear.
Everyone knows that a scarf is (usually) a long piece
of material of varying width that is wrapped around
the neck either as an accent piece or for warmth. But
when you mention cowls, gaiters, and the like, things
get a little fuzzy. Here are a few handy definitions for
styles featured in this book.

Cowl The word cowl comes from the Latin and refers to a monk's hood. Today, most people think of a cowl as a neckline that drapes loosely around the neck, often in an exaggerated turtleneck shape. A cowl can be attached to a sweater, or, as in the projects in this book, stand alone. It doesn't get more classic, or chic, than a cowl.

Gaiter Perhaps the opposite of a cowl in shape, a gaiter is a high, tubular collar that fits closely around the neck. Popularized by skiers, gaiters are often made of basic wool or fleece. Recently, the fashion crowd has started exploring their virtues as well by tricking them out in luxury fibers.

Dickey The term dickey may raise a "fashion don't" flag, but it is actually a very useful article of clothing. A dickey is a type of collar that tucks into the front of a shirt or coat and creates a seamless barrier against wind and cold. Several of the designs in this book can be worn outside the coat or tucked in, dickey-style.

...AND COMBINATIONS...

Capelets & Ponchettes Think of these as cowls with an extension that covers the shoulders. In this collection, there's a simple checkboard cowl that has an asymmetric poncho add-on which does double duty by covering the shoulders and neck (see pages 94–97). There's also a superbulky design that conforms to the shoulders and neck at once (see pages 14–17).

Snood Yes, a snood once referred to a sort of bag that was pinned or tied at the back of the head to hold long hair—a hairnet, if you will—but today's fashion houses and fashionistas are touting snoods as the latest in style. A modern snood drapes around the neck, like a cowl, and can be pulled up over the head to create a hood—perfect for when you want to go incognito.

Infinity Scarf Also called an "eternity loop" or a "circle scarf", an infinity scarf is a long cowl that seems to go on, if not forever, at least for a very long time. Infinity scarves can be worn long, or wrapped double, or even triple! Skim through a gossip mag, and you're likely to see several celebs sporting infinity scarves.

all seasons
(page 70)

tiny bobbles
(page 98)

grand slam
(page 124)

poncho v
(page 94)

just fur fun
(page 102)

northern lights
(page 14)

thick & thin
(page 46)

uptown girl
(page 30)

Donut A donut is essentially a neckpiece shaped like, well, a donut! Similar to a gaiter with its upright shape, a donut is usually larger and is often knit as a tube for double the thickness. Think of it as a muff for the neck!

SIZE MATTERS (when it comes to cowls and gaiters)

Cowls drape around the neck in folds, and to create this effect the circumference of a cowl usually has to be at least 24 inches (61cm). With this much length you also need some height; as a rule of thumb, start with at least 8 inches (20cm). Gaiters have an upright structure that clings to the neck. Traditional gaiters, like those worn for skiing, are usually 22 inches (56cm) in circumference and 10 to 12 inches (25–30cm) high. However, they can be tighter as long as they still fit over the head, and the height measurement can be varied according to the design and wearer.

BUILD-A-COWL WORKSHOP

Cowls and gaiters can be knit in three basic ways: 1) flat and seamed, 2) in the round, and 3) as a tube that is seamed.

Method 1: Seams to Me

This is the most basic construction method: Create a flat, two-dimensional piece of material by knitting back and forth, as you would make a scarf, then seam the ends together. This technique works for long or short cowls. It's an easy approach, but, unless you are a brand-new knitter, why would you bother with a seam? Consider the next two ways.

Method 2: Going 'Round and 'Round

In this method, you start by establishing the entire length of the piece. Using a long circular needle, cast on the number of stitches needed to get the entire circumference of the finished cowl. Join and work upward to establish the height. This is actually the simplest way to construct a cowl, as you don't have to join any seams when you're done knitting. It couldn't be easier.

Method 3: Totally Tubular

The third, perhaps least intuitive, method starts by establishing the entire width of the

Choose a shape, any shape

Cowls can be short...

piece. With a circular needle or double-pointed needles, cast on the number of stitches needed to form the circumference of a tube that will equal the height of the finished cowl. Work the tube in the round until you reach the desired length (i.e., the circumference of the cowl). For this method you will need to join the tube ends—not ideal as we like to avoid seams—but the BIG advantage is that you create a doubled-up fabric that gives body to the piece and provides an extra layer of warmth.

FIBER FACTS

Any kind of yarn can be used to knit gaiters and cowls, but the success of any project lies in picking the right yarn for the particular structure. Cowls—by definition and nature—drape, so consider yarns that drape as well, such as soft wool, cotton, silk, bamboo, mohair and linen. Gaiters, on the other hand, need some heft to establish their upright structure. That can be achieved no doubt with wool, even mohair. It can also be achieved with softer yarns like silk, linen and bamboo if the gaiter is made higher than usual. And, consider the function as well as the form. Braving an ice storm and wintry weather requires wool (and lots of it). In warmer months, you might want coverage without the insulation, so try linen, a perennial favorite.

...or long.

Method 1

First, knit a flat rectangle.

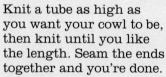

Next, join the ends and seam together. Voilà, instant cowl!

Method 2

Cast on to create the circumference, then keep knitting until the cowl is as high as you want it. No-sew perfection!

Method 3

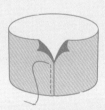

Knit a tube as high as you want your cowl to be, then knit until you like the length. Seam the ends together and you're done.

Gaiters are always short so that they hug the neck.

northern lights

The polar vortex is no match for this voluptuous cowl! A small stitch count and a handful of rounds mean superior warmth on the very coldest days.

northern lights

■■■□

WHAT YOU NEED
Yarn
Super Soft Alpaca **by North Light Fibers,
approx 130yd/119m hanks (alpaca/soy
silk/bamboo)** (**7**)
• **1 hank in ombre black/grey/creme (A)
for size Small/Medium**
• **1 hank in blue ombre (B) for size Large/
X-Large**

Needles
• **One each size 15 (10mm) circular
needles, 20"/50cm, 32"/80cm, and
40"/100cm long** or size to obtain gauge

Notions
• **4 stitch markers**
• **Size H/8 (5mm) crochet hook**

SIZES
To fit sizes Small/Medium (Large/X-Large).

ROVING COWL
The fabulous yarn used for this cowl made
it not just fun to make, but scrumptious
to wear. I recommend using a size 15 US
needle even though a size 19 might work
better—size 15 holds this rambunctious
yarn tight. Splurge and go for that super
soft lux skein of alpaca/soy silk/bamboo!

FINISHED MEASUREMENTS
Neck circumference
18½ (21½)"/47 (54.5)cm
Lower edge circumference
42½ (52)"/108 (132)cm
Length from shoulder (to lower edge)
10 (12)"/25.5 (30.5)cm

GAUGE
5 sts and 8 rnds = 4"/10cm over seed st
using size 15 (10mm) needle.
Take time to check gauge.

NOTE
The ombre grey/black/white cowl is shown
worked in size Small/Medium and the blue
ombre cowl is shown worked in size Large/
X-Large. Beg with the shortest circular
needle and change to the consecutive larger
circular needles when the sts will not fit
comfortably on the working circular needle.

SEED STITCH
(over an odd number of sts)
Rnd 1 *K1, p1; rep from *, end k1.
Rnd 2 *P1, k1; rep from *, end p1.
Rep these 2 rnds for seed st.

COWL
Beg at neck edge with shortest circular
needle and A (B), cast on 23 (27) sts. Join to
work in rnds, taking care not to twist sts,
and pm to mark beg of rnd. Work in seed st
for 4"/10cm.
Next rnd Knit.

Set-up rnd Shoulder Edge–k2, pm;
Back–k8 (10), pm; Shoulder Edge–k2, pm;
Front–k11 (13).
Begin Yoke Increases
Inc rnd 1 K1, M1, k1, sl marker; k1, M1,
k to 1 st before next marker, M1, k1, sl
marker; k1, M1, k1, sl marker; k1, M1, k
to 1 st before end, M1, k1—6 sts inc'd and
29 (33) sts on needle.
Rnd 2 Knit.
Inc rnd 3 K1, M1, k1, M1, k1, sl marker;
k1, M1, k to 1 st before next marker, M1,
k1, sl marker; k1, M1, k1, M1, k1, sl
marker, k1, M1, k to 1 st before end, M1,
k1—8 sts inc'd and 37 (41) sts on needle.
Rnd 4 Knit.
Inc rnd 5 K1, M1, k3, M1, k1, sl marker;
k1, M1, k to 1 st before next marker, M1,
k1, sl marker; k1, M1, k3, M1, sl marker;
k1, M1, k to 1 st before end, M1, k1—8 sts
inc'd and 45 (49) sts on needle.
Rnd 6 Knit.
Inc rnd 7 K1, M1, k5, M1, k1, sl marker;
k1, M1, k to 1 st before next marker, M1,
k1, sl marker; k1, M1, k5, M1, k1, sl
marker; k1, M1, k to 1 st before end, M1,
k1—8 sts inc'd and 53 (57) sts on needle.
Rnd 8 Knit.

Size Large/X-Large only
Inc rnd 9 K1, M1, k7, M1, k1, sl marker;
k1, M1, k to 1 st before next marker, M1,
k1, sl marker; k1, M1, k7, M1, k1, sl
marker; k1, M1, k to 1 st before end, M1,
k1—8 sts inc'd and 65 sts on needle.

For Both Sizes
Knit 1 (2) rnds more.
Then, work even in seed st for 5 (7)"/12.5
(18)cm more. Bind off in seed st pat.

FINISHING
Weave in ends on the WS.✤

sun valley

Take a cue from the ski set and make this sleek, double-faced cowl that fits close to the neck or pulls up over the ears for an instant wide headband.

sun valley

■■■□

WHAT YOU NEED

Yarn

Erin Worsted 3-Ply **by Imperial Yarn, 4oz/113g hanks, each approx 225yd/206m (wool)** (4)
• **1 hank each in #02 pearl gray (A) and #352 heart red (B)**

Needles
• **One size 7 (4.5mm) circular needle, 24"/60cm long** or size to obtain gauges

Notions
• **Stitch marker**
• **Tapestry needle**

SMOCK STITCH GAITER

This cowl is a classic gaiter shape yet it's the smock stitch pattern in contrasting colors that provides interest. Smock stitching looks as if the overlay is embroidered rather than knitted. A cowl is a nice way to give this technique a try.

FINISHED MEASUREMENTS

Circumference 21½"/54.5cm
Height 5¼"/13.5cm

GAUGES

18 sts and 27 rnds = 4"/10cm over St st using size 7 (4.5mm) needle.
18 sts and 40 rnds = 4"/10cm over 2-color smock stitch using size 7 (4.5mm) needle.
Take time to check gauges.

NOTE

This cowl is worked in a doubled-fabric thickness, with plain St st in A worked for the inside fabric and 2-color smock stitch on the outside surface. To beg working the cowl, the piece starts at the center edge of the inside fabric and works half the inside fabric, then the outside surface, then the 2nd half of the inside fabric. The cowl is then finished by seaming the cast-on edge to the bind-off edge.

2-COLOR SMOCK STITCH

(over a multiple of 4 sts)
Set-up rnd With A, knit.
Rnd 1 With B, *k1, sl 3 wyif; rep from * around.
Rnd 2 With A, knit.
Rnd 3 With A, k2, *insert the RH needle under the slipped B yarn from 2 rnds below and then k the next st on LH needle through this loop for 1 smock st, k3; rep from *

around, end with 1 smock st, then slip this last st from RH needle back to LH needle and replace the marker in this new position.
Rnd 4 With B, *sl 3 wyif, k1; rep from * around.
Rnd 5 With A, knit.
Rnd 6 With A, k1, *work 1 smock st, k3; rep from * around, end with 1 smock st, k2, then k the first st of next rnd and replace the marker in this new position. Rep rnds 1–6 for 2-color smock stitch.

COWL

Beg at the inside edge, with A, cast on 96 sts. Join, taking care not to twists sts, and pm to mark beg of rnd.
Knit 1 rnd, purl 1 rnd, knit 1 rnd.
Then knit 17 rnds more for the first half of the inside fabric.

Beg 2-Color Smock Stitch
First 2 rnds With B, knit.
Then, beg with set-up rnd, work in 2-color smock stitch for a total of 8 reps of the 6-rnd rep. Then, work rnds 1–5 once more.
Next rnd With B, M1, *work 1 smock st, k3; rep from * around, end with 1 smock st, k2.
Knit 1 rnd more with B. Cut B and cont with A to end of piece.
Complete the 2nd half of the inside fabric as foll:
Knit 17 rnds. Then, purl 1 rnd, knit 1 rnd. Bind off knitwise.

FINISHING

Weave in ends on the WS. Then fold the cast-on edge to meet the bind-off edge and seam tog from the RS of work using mattress st until all sts are joined. Fold cowl back so that the seam is on the center edge of the inside fabric as seen in photo.❖

café au lait

Two contrasting colors combine with a slanting ripple pattern
in this bubbly cowl. Your morning commute never looked so good.

café au lait

■■□□

WHAT YOU NEED

Yarn
Big Wool **by Rowan, 3½oz/100g skeins, each approx 87yd/80m (wool)** (6)
• **2 skeins each in #071 stag (A) and #001 white hot (B)**

Needles
• **One size 10½ (6.5mm) circular needle, 29"/74cm long** or size to obtain gauge

Notions
• **Stitch marker**
• **Tapestry needle**

RIPPLE COWL

This chunky, two-tone cowl is designed to be a simple (but exuberant) mix of color and texture. Gradual, neck-to-shoulder sizing combines with a ripple stitch for a sculpted look and a cozy feel. Alternating two colors creates bold interest.

FINISHED MEASUREMENTS

Shoulder circumference 35"/89cm
Neck circumference 22"/56cm
Height 10"/25.5cm

GAUGE

12 sts and 10 rnds = 4"/10cm over ripple pat st using size 10½ (6.5mm) needle.
Take time to check gauge.

COWL

With A, cast on 105 sts. Join, taking care not to twist sts, and pm to mark beg of rnd. Knit 1 rnd with A, purl 1 rnd with B, knit 1 rnd with A.
Beg ripple pattern
Rnd 1 With A, *(k2tog) 7 times, [k1, yo] 7 times; rep from * four times more.

Rnd 2 With B, purl.
Rnd 3 With B, knit.
Rnd 4 With A, purl.
Rnd 5 With A, *(k2tog) 7 times, [k1, yo] 7 times; rep from * four times more.
Rnd 6 With B, knit.
Rnd 7 With B, knit.
Rnd 8 With A, knit.
Rnds 9–44 Rep rnds 1–8 for ripple pat for 4 more reps. Then, work rnds 1–4 once more.
Beg top edge
Rnd 1 With A, knit.
Rnd 2 With B, purl.
Rnd 3 With A, (k2tog) 52 times, end k1—53 sts.
Rnd 4 With B, knit.
With B, bind off loosely knitwise.

FINISHING

Weave in ends on the WS.❖

street smart

Effortless downtown cool will be yours in this versatile zippered cowl.
Pair it with your favorite coat or jacket for a great night out.

street smart

WHAT YOU NEED

Yarn
Sebago **by Knit One, Crochet Too,**
1¾oz/50g skeins, each approx 146yd/133m
(wool) (**3**)
 • **4 skeins in #581 silver fern**

Needles
 • **One size 5 (3.75mm) circular needle,**
24"/60cm long or size to obtain gauge

Notions
 • **Tapestry needle (blunt point)**
 • **Tapestry needle (sharp point)**
 • **One 10"/25cm length close-end heavy**
metal zipper in black
 • **Straight pins**

RIB & ZIP COWL

Talk about a cowl collar for the ages! This classic can be worn outside a coat or tucked in for added warmth. And although it's knit here in wool, consider cotton and silk blends for warmer climates and seasons. A simple, flat piece of knitting, this cowl requires no additional shaping.

FINISHED MEASUREMENTS

Circumference (unstretched) 24"/61cm
Height 9½"/24cm

GAUGE

33 sts and 34 rows = 4"/10cm over picot rib, unstretched, using size 5 (3.75mm) needle.
Take time to check gauge.

PICOT RIB

(over a multiple of 4 sts plus 2)
Row 1 (RS) K2, *p2, k2; rep from * to end.
Row 2 P2, *k2, p2; rep from * to end.
Rows 3 and 4 Rep rows 1 and 2.
Row 5 Rep row 1.
Picot row 6 (WS) *P2, k2tog, yo; rep from
*, end p2.
Rep rows 1–6 for picot rib.

K2, P2 RIB

(over a multiple of 4 sts plus 2)
Row 1 (RS) K2, *p2, k2; rep from * to end.
Row 2 P2, *k2, p2; rep from * to end.
Rep these 2 rows for k2, p2 rib.

COWL

Beg at the cowl center, cast on 198 sts.
Working back and forth in rows, work even in picot rib for 10"/25.5cm.
Then, work even in k2, p2 rib for 10"/25.5cm more. Bind off in rib.

FINISHING

Do not block or press finished piece.
Zipper
Fold the knitted piece in half lengthwise, with RS facing, so that the cast-on edge meets the bind-off edge. Seam these 2 edges together, matching the sts and taking care that the seam remains elastic. This creates a tube with the seam worn around the neck (see photo).

Line up the sides (along the rows) of this tube together and lay the zipper into this opening. Using straight pins, pin the zipper in place being sure that the zipper "teeth" are cleared and the regular rib and picot rib match at the center.

Carefully sew zipper in place securely using the sharp point tapestry needle and yarn, with a running stitch. Once in place, sew the cowl tog at the lower zipper base for ½"/1.25cm at the front edge and ½"/1.25cm at the back. This will secure the zipper in place. Weave in ends on the WS.✤

uptown girl

A must-have accessory for any wardrobe, this faux fur and lace cowl takes all your basics upscale. It's incredibly fun to knit, too!

uptown girl

■■■□

WHAT YOU NEED

Yarn
Akiko **by Louisa Harding Yarns,
1¾oz/50g hanks, each approx 98yd/90m
(wool/alpaca)** 🄸
• **2 hanks in #6 slate (A)**
Luzia **by Louisa Harding Yarns,
1¾oz/50g balls, each approx 43yd/40m
(viscose/nylon)** 🄶
• **2 balls in #7 otter (B)**
Orielle **by Louisa Harding Yarns,
1¾oz/50g hanks each approx 120yd/110m
(baby alpaca/metallic polyamide)** 🄳
• **1 hank in #1 white (C)**

Needles
• **One each sizes 10½ and 11 (6.5 and
8mm) circular needles, 16"/40cm long** or
size to obtain gauges
• **One set (5) size 5 (3.75mm) double-pointed
needles (dpns)**

Notions
• **Stitch markers**
• **Tapestry needles**

CONTRAST COWL
The contrast of knitting with two vastly
different yarn types makes this cowl a fun
and interesting project. Complementing
the fur section is a soft, metallic alpaca
that subtly 'ups' the glamour quotient.
An alternate idea is to replace the fur with
a textured bulky weight yarn.

FINISHED MEASUREMENTS
Circumference 17"/43cm
Height 9"/23cm

GAUGES
11 sts and 16 rnds = 4"/10cm over St st
using 1 rnd of 2 strands of A held tog and
size 10½ (6.5mm) needle, alternated with
1 rnd of 1 strand of B and size 11 (8mm)
needle.
22 sts and 30 rnds = 4"/10cm over
chart pat using 1 strand of C and size 5
(3.75mm) dpns.
Take time to check gauges.
Note When working with A, use a double
strand of A and use size 10½ (6.5mm)
needle. Work in B using a single strand of
B and size 11 (8mm) needle. Work with C
foll chart using a single strand of C and
size 5 (3.75mm) dpns.

COWL
With 2 strands of A and size 10½ (6.5mm)
needle, cast on 48 sts. Join, taking care not
to twist sts, and pm to mark beg of rnd.

Rnd 1 With size 10½ (6.5mm) needle and 2
strands of A, knit.
Rnd 2 With size 11 (8mm) needle and 1
strand of B, knit.
Rep rnds 1 and 2 for the section in fur
until piece measures 20"/51cm from beg,
end with pat rnd 1. Cut yarns A and B.

Beg Chart Pattern
Change to dpns and work as foll:
Rnd 1 With 1 strand of C, [k12 onto 1 dpn]
4 times.
Rnd 2 *Kfb; rep from * around—24 sts on
each dpn for a total of 96 sts.
Rnd 3 Knit.
Rnd 4 Purl.
Rnd 5 Knit.
Rnd 6 Work two 12-st reps of rnd 1 of
chart on each of the 4 dpn.
Rnds 7–42 Cont in chart as established
for a total of six 6-rnd reps.
Rnd 43 Knit.
Rnd 44 Purl.
Rnds 45 and 46 Knit.
Bind off knitwise.

FINISHING
Thread C onto tapestry needle and join the
bound-off edge to the cast-on edge seaming
every other st in C to a single st in the cast-
on edge in A. Weave in ends on the WS.✣

12-st rep

Stitch Key

☐ knit

☑ yo

⟋ k2tog

⟍ SKP

30–love

Make your move in this eye-catching cowl! Bright colors and bold lines
pair up for a winning look that's both warm and sporty.

30–love

■■□□

RIBBED COWL
Go for the grand slam in this sporty cowl. The crisp lines make it eye-catching and the ribs give it plenty of stretch for an easy (but snug) fit. Using three coordinating colors, it's the perfect cowl for just about anyone.

FINISHED MEASUREMENTS
Circumference 20"/51cm
Height (with collar folded) 7"/18cm

GAUGE
22 sts and 26 rnds = 4"/10cm over k2, p2 rib, slightly stretched, using size 5 (3.75mm) needle.
Take time to check gauge.

K2, P2 RIB
(over a multiple of 4 sts)
Rnd 1 *K2, p2; rep from * around.
Rep rnd 1 for k2, p2 rib.

COWL
Beg at the top edge with B, cast on 112 sts. Join to work in rnds, taking care not to twist sts, and pm to mark beg of rnd.
Rnds 1–8 Work even in k2, p2 rib. Cut B.

Rnd 9 With A, knit.
Rnds 10–12 Work in k2, p2 rib.
Rnd 13 With C, knit.
Rnd 14 With C, work in k2, p2 rib. Cut C.
Rnd 15 With A, knit.
Cont with A in k2, p2 rib until piece measures 10"/25.5cm from beg. Then, change from RS to WS (for the collar turnback) as foll:
Next rnd Wrap the last p st on the RH needle of the previous rnd (as for a short-row wrap) and turn the work to the WS and work this rnd in the changed (RS becomes WS) direction by *k1, M1, k1, p2; rep from * around—140 sts.
Rnds 2–4 *K3, p2; rep from * around.
Rnd 5 With C, knit.
Rnds 6–8 *K3, p2; rep from * around. Cut C.
Rnd 9 With A, knit.
Rnds 10–13 With A, k3, p2; rep from * around.
Bind off in rib.

FINISHING
Weave in ends on the WS (being sure that the WS of the collar turnback is in place as the WS).❖

it takes two

A classic cowl design (with a twist) and a cozy hat make this an easy project for all knitting levels. Delight in the simple elegance of this sweet duo!

it takes two

■■□□

WHAT YOU NEED

Yarn

Magnolia **by Classic Elite Yarns,**
1¾oz/50g skeins, each approx
120yd/110m (wool/silk) 🔢
- **5 skeins in #5419 petal**

Needles
- **One size 6 (4mm) circular needle,**
16"/40cm long or size to obtain gauge
- **One set (2) size 6 (4mm) double-pointed**
needles (dpns)

Notions
- **3 stitch markers**
- **Tapestry needle**

TAB COWL & HAT

Asymmetric garments offer contrast and
interest. The added tab on the cowl loops
around the cowl and is knotted through
itself for a fun take on a classic design!

FINISHED MEASUREMENTS

Cowl
- **Circumference** 22"/56cm
- **Height** 12"/30.5cm

Hat
- **Circumference** 19"/48cm
- **Height (with band folded up)** 11"/28cm

GAUGE

21 sts and 30 rnds = 4"/10cm over
double moss stitch worked in rnds using
size 6 (4mm) needle.
Take time to check gauge.

COWL

K2, P2 RIB

(worked in rnds over a multiple of 4 sts)
Rnd 1 *K2, p2; rep from * around.
Rep rnd 1 for k2, p2 rib.

DOUBLE MOSS STITCH

(worked in rnds over a multiple of 4 sts)
Rnds 1 and 2 *K2, p2; rep from * around.
Rnds 3 and 4 *P2, k2; rep from * around.
Rep rnds 1–4 for double moss st.

COWL

Beg at the top edge, cast on 120 sts. Join to
work in rnds, taking care not to twist sts,
and pm to mark beg of rnd.
Rnds 1–5 Work in k2, p2 rib.
Rnd 6 Knit.
Begin Double Moss Stitch
Work in double moss st until piece
measures 11½"/29cm from beg.
Lower rib band
Rnd 1 Knit.
Rnds 2–6 Work in k2, p2 rib.
Rnd 7 Bind off 98 sts, then work in rib
across the rem 22 sts in rows as foll:
Row 1 (RS) K2, [p2,k2] 5 times.
Row 2 (WS) [P2, k2] 5 times, p2.
Rep last 2 rows for 18"/45.5cm for the
strap. Bind off in rib.

FINISHING

Weave in ends on the WS.

HAT

K2, P2 RIB

(worked in rnds over a multiple of 4 sts)
Rnd 1 *K2, k2; rep from * around.
Rep rnd 1 for k2, p2 rib.

DOUBLE MOSS STITCH

(worked in rnds over a multiple of 4 sts)
Rnds 1 and 2 *K2, p2; rep from * around.
Rnds 3 and 4 *P2, k2; rep from * around.
Rep rnds 1–4 for double moss st.

HAT

Beg at the lower edge with circular needle,
cast on 100 sts. Join to work in rnds,
taking care not to twist sts, and pm to
mark beg of rnd. Work in k2, p2 rib for
6"/15cm.
Next rnd Knit.
Begin Double Moss Stitch
Work in double moss st until piece
measures 13"/33cm from beg.
Shape crown
Next rnd Work 50 sts in double moss st,
pm, work 50 sts in double moss st.
Dec rnd 1 K2tog, work in double moss st to
2 sts before marker, ssk, sl marker, k2tog,
work in double moss st to last 2 sts of rnd,
ssk—4 sts dec'd and 96 sts.
Rnd 2 Work even in double moss st.
Rep the last 2 rnds 8 times more—64 sts.

FINISHING

Turn hat inside out. Divide sts evenly
onto 2 dpns, divided with 32 sts between
markers on each dpn. Then, using the
circular needle, close the top using 3-needle
bind-off method (see page 141). Weave in
ends on the WS.❖

on the go

Get going with this clever and sporty pocketed cowl!
Featuring a topstitched zipper, it's just right when you're on the move.

on the go

WHAT YOU NEED

Yarn
Worsted Hand Dyes **by Blue Sky Alpacas**, 3½oz/100g hanks, each approx 100yd/91m **④**
• **1 hank in #2003 ecru (A)**
• **2 hanks in #2025 charcoal (B)**

Needles
• **One size 9 (5.5mm) circular needle, 24"/60cm long** or size to obtain gauges

Notions
• **3 stitch markers**
• **Tapestry needle**
• **One 6"/15cm heavyweight closed end zipper in black (source: zipit@etsy.com)**
• **Straight pins**

POCKET COWL

I love a "secret compartment" design! The first Cowl Girls collection had one with button closures, so it was time for a zipper. The zipper is placed on the top side and fastened with a backward stitch for a fun design element. Or you can wear it with the zipper facing inward so the secret is just for you!

FINISHED MEASUREMENTS

Circumference (at edges) 24½"/62cm
(at center) 23"/58.5cm
Height 7"/18cm

GAUGES

15 sts and 22 rows = 4"/10cm over St st using size 9 (5.5mm) needle.
14 sts and 24 rows = 4"/10cm over seed st using size 9 (5.5mm) needle.
Take time to check gauges.

SEED STITCH

(worked over an even number of sts)
Row 1 *K1, p1; rep from * to end.
Row 2 *P2, k1; rep from * to end.
Rep rows 1 and 2 for seed st.

NOTE

Cowl is worked back and forth in rows beg at the center edge with A (for the split opening that holds the zipper), then worked around to the seed st edge in B, the seed st lining in B, the opposite seed st edge in B, and finally the 2nd half of the A section.

COWL

First section in A
With A, cast on 86 sts. Working back and forth in rows, work as foll:
Row 1 (RS) With A, knit.
Rows 2–7 Rep row 1.
Row 8 With A, purl.
Row 9 With A, knit.
Rows 10–13 Rep rows 8 and 9 twice more.
Row 14 With A, purl. Cut A, join B.

Seed Stitch Section
With B, work as foll:
Row 1 (RS) With B, knit.
Cont with B, work in seed st for 10"/25.5cm. Cut B, join A.

Second Section in A
Row 1 (RS) With A, knit.
Row 2 With A, purl.
Rows 3–8 Rep rows 1 and 2 three times more.
Rows 9–14 With A, knit.
Bind off knitwise with A.

FINISHING

Lay the piece flat and fold up the cast-on edge to meet the bind-off edge at the center for the zipper placement. Along this line, pm at 5"/12.5cm from the right hand edge, then a 2nd marker at 5"/12.5cm from the first marker, then a 3rd marker at 5"/12.5cm from the 2nd marker (see schematic diagram). The space between the 2nd and 3rd marker will determine the zipper opening (red line on schematic). Using tapestry needle with A, seam the cowl center along the 5"/12.5cm at one side and leave the 13"/3cm at the other side free to be seamed later.

To insert the zipper, lay the zipper centered along the opening with the "teeth" extending slightly over the cast-on/bind-off edges, pin in place with straight pins. Then, using tapestry needle with A, use a running back stitch worked on the RS to secure entire zipper on one edge (working stitch by stitch into the knitted sts). Then, work the other edge in same way.

Seam the other 13"/33cm at the other side of the zipper as before and reinforce each side of the zipper using extra sts. To close the cowl and form a tube, sew the side edges tog using mattress st from the RS. Weave in ends on the WS.✤

DIAGRAM

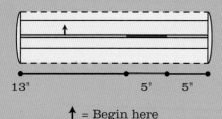

13"   5"   5"

↑ = Begin here

thick & thin

Cool color tones set up the mood for these two coordinating cowls
that can be worn separately or together.

thick & thin

■■■□

WHAT YOU NEED
Yarn
Longwood **by Cascade Yarns, 3½oz/100g skeins, each approx 191yd/175m (wool)** (4)
• **1 skein each in #18 green spruce (A) and #20 cyan (C)**
Magnum **by Cascade Yarns, 8.82oz/250g skeins, each approx 123yd/112m (wool)** (6)
• **1 skein each in #9464 blueberry (B) and #9550 mediterranean heather (D)**

Needles
Long Cowl
• **One each sizes 7 and 13 (4.5 and 9mm) circular needles, 32"/80cm long** or size to obtain gauge.
Short Cowl
• **One each sizes 7 and 13 (4.5 and 9mm) circular needles, 24"/60cm long** or size to obtain gauge.

Notions
• **Stitch marker**
• **Tapestry needle**

DROP STITCH COWL DUO
Intentionally dropping stitches is great fun and can create interesting patterns and designs. Using a bulky gauge yarn, you'll be delighted by the bubbly, loopy texture that is formed in the space from the dropped stitch. A simple, minimal pattern showcases the exuberance of the "bulky drop."

FINISHED MEASUREMENTS
Long Cowl
• **Neck circumference** 48"/122cm
• **Height** 7"/18cm
Short Cowl
• **Neck circumference** 26"/66cm
• **Height** 11"/28cm

GAUGES
16 sts and 26 rnds = 4"/10cm over garter st using A and smaller needle.
8 sts and 11 rnds = 4"/10cm over drop st using B and larger needle.
Take time to check gauges.

LONG COWL

GARTER STITCH
(over any numer of sts)
Rnd 1 Knit.
Rnd 2 Purl.
Rep rnds 1 and 2 for garter st.

COWL
With smaller needle and A, cast on 200 sts. Join, taking care not to twist sts, and pm to mark beg of rnd.
Rnds 1–4 Work in garter st.
Rnd 5 Knit.

Beg Drop Stitch
Rnd 1 Using smaller needle and B, k2tog around—100 sts.
Change to larger needle.
Rnds 2 and 3 Knit.
Rnd 4 *K1, M1; rep from * around—200 sts.
Rnd 5 *K1, drop 1 st from needle; rep from * around—100 sts.
Rnd 6 Knit.
Rnd 7 Kfb in each st around—200 sts.
Change to smaller needle and A.
Rnd 8 Knit, pulling each st firmly to even out the sts.
Rnd 9 Purl, pulling each st firmly to even out the sts.
Rnds 10 and 11 Rep rnds 8 and 9.
Rep rnds 1–11 once more.
Then, knit 1 rnd, purl 1 rnd. Bind off knitwise.

FINISHING
Weave in ends on the WS.

SHORT COWL

GARTER STITCH
(over any numer of sts)
Rnd 1 Knit.
Rnd 2 Purl.
Rep rnds 1 and 2 for garter st.

COWL
With smaller needle and C, cast on 100 sts. Join, taking care not to twist sts, and pm to mark beg of rnd.
Rnds 1–4 Work in garter st.
Rnd 5 Knit.

Beg Drop Stitch
Rnd 1 Using smaller needle and D, k2tog around—50 sts.
Change to larger needle.
Rnd 2 Knit.
Rnd 3 *K1, M1; rep from * around—100 sts.
Rnd 4 *K1, drop 1 st from needle; rep from * around—50 sts.
Rnd 5 Kfb in each st around—100 sts.
Change to smaller needle and C.
Rnd 6 Knit, pulling each st firmly to even out the sts.
Rnd 7 Purl, pulling each st firmly to even out the sts.
Rnds 8 and 9 Rep rnds 6 and 7.
Rep rnds 1–9 four times more.
Then, knit 1 rnd, purl 1 rnd. Bind off knitwise.

FINISHING
Weave in ends on the WS.❖

a knitting romance

Bobbles, lace, openwork, and ribs are the many ways you can express your love of knitting in this extra-long, stitch mix cowl.

a knitting romance

■■■■

WHAT YOU NEED

Yarn
Chickadee **by Quince & Co,** 1¾oz/50g
hanks, each approx 181yd/166m (wool) (2)
• **3 hanks in #103 frost**

Needles
• **One size 4 (3.5mm) circular needle,
24"/60cm long** or size to obtain gauge
• **One set (4) size 4 (3.5mm) double-
pointed needles (dpns)**

Notions
• **Stitch marker**
• **Cable needle (cn)**
• **Tapestry needle**

RIOT COWL

This design is a joyous stroll through
eight all-time, workhorse stitch patterns.
Think of it as a knit sampler and a great
way to try your hand at a variety of
stitches. The piece begins at the lower
border or neck edge with a bobbled border
inspired by Turkish lacework.

FINISHED MEASUREMENTS

Circumference 24"/61cm
Height 17"/43cm

GAUGE

24 sts and 36 rnds = 4"/10cm over moss
stitch pattern using size 4 (3.5mm) needle.
Take time to check gauge.

STITCH GLOSSARY

MB4 (Make 4-st bobble) K into front, back,
front, and back of st, then with LH needle, pull
the first 3 sts over the last st, then k final st.
MB5 (Make 5-st bobble) K into front,
back, front, back, and front of st, then with
LH needle, pull the first 4 sts over the last
st, then k final st.
MB6 (Make 6-st bobble) [K into front and
back of st] 3 times, then with LH needle, pull
the first 5 sts over the last st, then k final st.
C6R Sl next 3 sts to cn and hold to back,
k3, then k3 from cn.
C6L Sl next 3 sts to cn and hold to front,
k3, then k3 from cn.

SEED STITCH

(over an even number of sts)
Rnd 1 *K1, p1; rep from * around.
Rnd 2 *P1, k1; rep from * around.
Rep rnds 1 and 2 for seed st.

MB6 PATTERN

(over a multiple of 6 sts)
Rnd 1 *K5, MB6; rep from * around.
Rnd 2 *K5, k1 tbl; rep from * around.

HORIZONTAL LACE PATTERN

(over an even number of sts)
Rnds 1 and 2 Purl.
Rnd 3 *Yo, SKP; rep from * around.
Rnds 4 and 5 Purl.

BAMBOO STITCH

(over an even number of sts)
Rnd 1 Knit.
Rnd 2 *Yo, k2, pass the yo over the k2; rep
from * around.
Rnds 3–6 Rep rnds 1 and 2 twice more.
Rnd 7 Knit.

MB5 PATTERN

(over a multiple of 4 sts)
Rnd 1 *K3, MB5; rep from * around.
Rnd 2 *K3, k1 tbl; rep from * around.

PICOT PATTERN

(over an even number of sts)
Rnds 1–5 Knit.
Rnd 6 *K the 2nd st on LH needle, then k
the first st and sl both sts off needle tog,
then sl the first st over the 2nd st, yo; rep
from * around.
Rnds 7–11 Knit.

MOSS STITCH

(over a multiple of 4 sts)
Rnds 1 and 2 *K2, p2; rep from * around.
Rnds 3 and 4 *P2, k2; rep from * around.
Rnds 5–10 Rep rnds 1–4 once then rnds 1
and 2 once more.

VANDYKE STITCH #1

(over a multiple of 8 sts)
Rnd 1 *K5, yo, k2tog, k1; rep from * around.
Rnds 2, 4, and 6 Knit.
Rnd 3 *K3, k2tog tbl, yo, k1, yo, k2tog;
rep from * around.
Rnd 5 K1, *k1, k2tog tbl, yo, k3, yo, k2tog;
rep from * around, end by working last
rep as follows: *k1, k2tog tbl, yo, k3, yo,

sl 1, then remove beg marker and sl 1 from the beg of next row to the other side of marker, then k2tog the 2 slipped sts at the end of the row.

Rnd 7 *MB4, k7; rep from * around.
Rnd 8 *K1 tbl, k7; rep from * around.

DROP STITCH CABLES
(over a multiple of 12 sts)
Rnd 1 Knit, wrapping yarn 3 times around needle for each st.
Rnd 2 Sl each st, unwrapping each wrap to elongate all of the sts.
Rnd 3 *C6R, C6L; rep from * around.
Rnd 4 Knit.
Rnd 5 Purl.

VANDYKE STITCH #2
(over a multiple of 8 sts)
Rnd 1 *MB4, k7; rep from * around.
Rnd 2 *K1 tbl, k7; rep from * around.
Rnd 3 *K1, yo, k2tog, k3, k2tog tbl, yo; rep from * around
Rnd 4 Knit.
Rnd 5 *K2, yo, k2tog, k1, k2tog tbl, yo, k1; rep from * around
Rnds 6 and 7 Knit.
Rnds 8 and 9 Purl.

SEED STITCH RIB
(over an even number of sts)
Rnd 1 *K1, p1; rep from * around.
Rnd 2 Knit.
Rnds 3–8 Rep rnds 1 and 2 three times more.

K2, P2 RIB
(over a multiple of 4 sts)
Rnd 1 *K2, p2; rep from * around.
Rep rnd 1 for k2, p2 rib.

COWL
Edging
Note Use 2 dpns for edging.
BOBBLE CLUSTER
Make slipknot and place on dpn, *cast on 1 st—2 sts. Work back and forth in rows as foll:
Row 1 (RS) [K1, p1] twice into first st, k1—5 sts.
Rows 2, 4, 6, and 8 Sl 1, p4.
Rows 3, 5, and 7 Sl 1, k4.
Row 9 K2tog, k1, k2tog—3 sts.
Row 10 P3tog, turn, fold bobble in half with the WS tog. Insert RH needle into cast-on st and k it tog with the last st for bobble—1 st rem.
Rep from * twice more, slip final st to spare needle to work later, cut yarn—1 bobble cluster complete.
Make 11 bobble clusters separately. Do not cut yarn at end of final bobble cluster.
TRIANGLE
Note Use the rem stitch from each bobble cluster to start a triangle, beg with bobble cluster with yarn still attached. Cut yarn at end of each triangle except for the last. Slip each triangle to circular needle once complete.
Row 1 (RS) Yo, k1, yo.
Row 2 and all WS rows Purl.
Row 3 K1, yo, k1, yo, k1—5 sts.
Row 5 K1, yo, k3, yo, k1—7 sts.
Row 7 K1, yo, k5, yo, k1—9 sts.
Row 9 K1, yo, k7, yo, k1—11 sts.
Row 11 K1, yo, k9, yo, k1—13 sts.

Cowl
Rnd 1 Join triangles to work in rnds on circular needle by knitting 143 sts around, pm to mark beg of rnd.
Rnd 2 Purl.
Rnd 3 Kfb, knit to end of rnd—144 sts.
Rnds 4–7 Work in seed st.
Rnds 8 and 9 Knit.

Rnds 10 and 11 Work MB6 pattern.
Rnd 12 Knit.
Next 5 rnds Work horizontal lace pattern.
Next 7 rnds Work bamboo stitch.
Next 2 rnds Work MB5 pattern.
Knit 1 rnd, purl 1 rnd.
Next 11 rnds Work picot pattern.
Purl 1 rnd, knit 1 rnd.
Next 10 rnds Work moss stitch.
Knit 1 rnd.
Next 7 rnds Work bamboo stitch.
Next 2 rnds Work MB5 pattern.
Purl 1 rnd, knit 1 rnd.
Next 8 rnds Work Vandyke st #1.
Next 5 rnds Work horizontal lace pattern.
Knit 2 rnds.
Next 2 rnds Work MB6 pattern.
Knit 1 rnd, purl 1 rnd.
Next 5 rnds Work drop stitch cables.
Next 11 rnds Work picot pattern.
Purl 1 rnd.
Next 7 rnds Work bamboo stitch.
Knit 1 rnd.
Next 2 rnds Work MB6 pattern.
Knit 1 rnd, purl 1 rnd.
Next 10 rnds Work moss stitch.
Knit 1 rnd, purl 1 rnd, knit 1 rnd.
Next 8 rnds Work Vandyke st #2.
Next 2 rnds Work MB6 pattern.
Knit 1 rnd.
Next 8 rnds Work seed stitch rib.
Next 6 rnds [Purl 1 rnd, knit 1 rnd] 3 times for garter st.
Last 16 rnds Work in k2, p2 rib. Bind off in rib.

FINISHING
Weave in ends on the WS.✣

comfort zone

This paired-down version of wrapping yourself in an afghan on the couch is sure to turn heads when you leave the house and take it to the street.

comfort zone

■■■■

WHAT YOU NEED

Yarn
Liberty Wool **by Classic Elite Yarns,
1¾oz/50g balls, each approx 122yd/112m
(wool)** (4)
• **2 balls each in #7847 sky (A), #7892
pale blue (B), #7849 lapis (C), and #7879
midnight blue (D)**
• **1 ball each in #7813 ebony (E), #7858
scarlet (F), and #7827 wine (G)**

Needles
• **One set (5) size 7 (4.5mm) double-pointed
needles (dpns)** or size to obtain gauge
• **One each sizes 5 and 7 (3.75 and 4.5mm)
circular needles, 40"/100cm long**

Notions
• **Stitch marker**
• **Tapestry needle**

MOTIF COWL

This cowl turns tradition on its head.
Two motifs, using the same array of blue
tonal colors, combine with side panels of
contrasting stitches. Accents of scarlet,
black, and wine add interest. It's as cozy as
your grandmother's afghan but as chic as a
night on the town.

FINISHED MEASUREMENTS

Circumference 60"/152cm
Height 15"/38cm

GAUGE

One motif is 5"/12.5cm square using larger
needle.
Take time to check gauge.

STITCH GLOSSARY

1L St (1 long stitch) Use RH needle to go
into the next st three rows down, and pull
up a loop, knit next stitch, pass loop over
this st.

SEED STITCH

(over an even number of sts)
Rnd 1 *K1, p1; rep from * around.
Rnd 2 *P1, k1; rep from * around.
Rep rnds 1 and 2 for seed st.

COWL

Motif 1
(make 12, see diagram for color
combinations)
With MC and dpns, cast on 12 sts and
divide evenly onto 4 dpns with 3 sts on
each dpn. Join to work in rnds, taking care
not to twist sts, and pm to mark beg of rnd.
Rnd 1 Knit.
Rnd 2 [K1, yo, k1, yo, k1] 4 times—8 sts
inc'd and 20 sts.
Rnd 3 Knit.
Rnd 4 [K1, yo, k3, yo, k1] 4 times—8 sts
inc'd and 28 sts.
Rnd 5 *K1, p1, k3, p1, k1; rep from *
around.
Rnd 6 *K1, yo, p1, k3, p1, yo, k1; rep from
* around—8 sts inc'd and 36 sts.
Rnd 7 *K1, p2, k3, p2, k1; rep from
*around.
Rnd 8 *K1, yo, p2, k3, p2, yo, k1; rep from
* around—8 sts inc'd and 44 sts.
Rnd 9 *K1, p3, k3, p3, k1; rep from * around.
Rnd 10 *K1, yo, p3, k3, p3, yo, k1; rep
from * around—8 sts inc'd and 52 sts.
Rnd 11 *K2, p3, k3, p3, k2; rep from * around.
Rnd 12 *K1, yo, k1, p3, k3, p3, k1, yo, k1;
rep from * around—8 sts inc'd and 60 sts.
Rnd 13 *K3, p3, k3, p3, k3; rep from * around.
Rnd 14 *K1, yo, k2, p3, k3, p3, k2, yo, k1;
rep from * around—8 sts inc'd and 68 sts.
Rnd 15 *K4, p3, k3, p3, k4; rep from * around.
Rnd 16 *K1, yo, k3, p3, k3, p3, k3, yo, k1;
rep from * around—8 sts inc'd and 76 sts.
Rnd 17 *K1, p1, k3, p3, k3, p3, k3, p1, k1;
rep from * around.

Rnd 18 *K1, yo, p1, k3, p3, k3, p3, k3, p1, yo, k1; rep from * around—8 sts inc'd and 84 sts.
Rnd 19 *K1, p2, k3, p3, k3, p3, k3, p2, k1; rep from * around.
Cut MC, join CC.
Rnd 20 [K1, M1, k to 1 st before end of dpn, M1, k1] 4 times—92 sts.
Bind off knitwise.

Motif 2
(make 12, see diagram for color combinations)
With MC and dpns, cast on 12 sts and divide evenly onto 4 dpns with 3 sts on each dpn. Join to work in rnds, taking care not to twist sts, and pm to mark beg of rnd.
Rnd 1 Knit.
Rnd 2 [K1, yo, k1, yo, k1] 4 times—8 sts inc'd and 20 sts.
Rnd 3 Knit.
Rnd 4 *K1, yo, p3, yo, k1; rep from * around—8 sts inc'd and 28 sts.
Rnd 5 *K1, p5, k1; rep from * around.
Rnd 6 *K1, yo, p5, yo, k1; rep from * around—8 sts inc'd and 36 sts.
Rnd 7 Knit.
Rnd 8 *K1, yo, k7, yo, k1; rep from * around—8 sts inc'd and 44 sts.
Rnd 9 Knit.
Rnd 10 *K1, yo, p9, yo, k1; rep from * around—8 sts inc'd and 52 sts.
Rnd 11 *K1, p11, k1; rep from * around
Rnd 12 *K1, yo, p11, yo, k1; rep from * around—8 sts inc'd and 60 sts.
Rnd 13 Knit.
Rnd 14 *K1, yo, k13, yo, k1; rep from *

around—8 sts inc'd and 68 sts.
Rnd 15 Knit.
Rnd 16 *K1, yo, p15, yo, k1; rep from * around—8 sts inc'd and 76 sts.
Rnd 17 *K1, p17, k1; rep from * around.
Rnd 18 *K1, yo, p17, yo, k1; rep from * around—8 sts inc'd and 84 sts.
Rnd 19 Knit.
Cut MC, join CC.
Rnd 20 [K1, M1, k to 1 st before end of dpn, M1, k1] 4 times—92 sts.
Bind off knitwise.

CONSTRUCT COWL

Block squares. Lay out the squares on a table, foll the diagram for placement. Sew the squares together. Connect the ends of the scarf that is created.

Short Border

With RS facing, smaller circular needle and A, pick up and k 24 sts from each square along one long edge of piece for a total of 288 sts. Join to work in rnds and pm to mark beg of rnd. Change to larger circular needle.
Rnd 1 Purl.
Rnd 2 Knit.
Rnd 3 With C, knit.
Rnd 4 With D, knit.
Rnd 5 With F, *k3, 1L st; rep from * around.
Rnd 6 With A, knit.
Rnd 7 With G, knit.
Rnd 8 With B, knit.
Cut all colors except G, and cont with G to end of border as foll:
Rnds 9 and 10 Knit.

Rnds 11–13 Work in seed st.
Bind off in pat.

Long Border

Along opposite long edge, with RS facing, smaller circular needle and A, pick up and k 288 sts as for the first edge. Join. Change to larger circular needle and C.
Rnd 1 Knit.
Rnd 2 Purl.
Rnd 3 With B, knit.
Rnds 4 and 5 With G, knit.
Rnd 6 With F, *k1, 1L st; rep from * around.
Rnd 7 With F, knit.
Rnds 8 and 9 With D, knit.
Rnd 10 With E, knit.
Rnd 11 With B, *k3, 1L st; in next st; rep from * around.
Rnd 12 With E, knit.
Rnd 13 With A, knit.
Rnds 14–16 With C, knit.
Rnd 17 With A, knit.
Rnd 18 With F, *k2, 1L st, k1; rep from * around.
Rnds 19 and 20 With A, knit.
Cut all colors except B, and cont with B to end of border as foll:
Rnd 20 Knit.
Rnds 21–27 Work in seed st.
Bind off in pat.

FINISHING

Weave in ends on the WS.✤

M2 MC = C CC = E	M1 MC = D CC = G	M2 MC = B CC = F	M1 MC = A CC = G	M2 MC = C CC = F	M2 MC = B CC = E	M2 MC = A CC = F	M2 MC = C CC = G	M1 MC = D CC = F	M1 MC = A CC = E	M2 MC = B CC = G	M1 MC = A CC = F
M1 MC = B CC = G	M1 MC = C CC = F	M1 MC = D CC = E	M1 MC = B CC = F	M2 MC = A CC = E	M2 MC = D CC = G	M1 MC = C CC = E	M1 MC = B CC = E	M2 MC = A CC = G	M2 MC = D CC = F	M1 MC = C CC = G	M2 MC = D CC = E

Key
M1 = Motif 1
M2 = Motif 2

Colors for MC
A = Sky
B = Pale blue
C = Lapis
D = Midnight blue

Colors for CC
E = Ebony
F = Scarlet
G = Wine

sweet treats

Abundant proportions and a bumpy, dimensional surface make this cowl a deliciously cozy confection. Bundle up!

sweet treats

■■■□

WHAT YOU NEED

Yarn
Cashmerino Aran **by Debbie Bliss/KFI,
1¾oz/50g balls, each approx 98yd/90m**
(wool/acrylic/cashmere) (⁴)
• **4 balls in #27 stone (A)**
• **4 balls in #25 white (B)**

Needles
• **One size 7 (4.5mm) circular needle,
32"/80cm long** or size to obtain gauge

Notions
• **Stitch marker**
• **Cable needle (cn)**
• **Tapestry needle**

FROSTING COWL

Let them eat cake! This homage to the
wedding cake is composed of cellular
lace & half-cables. Two colors alternate
between the patterns and half-cables switch
direction with the colors. Densely worked
cables create a smocking effect in the mid-
section while the final section tapers for a
flattering wrap and drape.

FINISHED MEASUREMENTS

Circumference (at lower edge) 46"/117cm
          (at neck edge) 24"/61cm
Height 14"/35.5cm

GAUGE

22 sts and 28 rnds = 4"/10cm over cellular
stitch using size 7 (4.5mm) needle.
Take time to check gauge.

STITCH GLOSSARY

6-st RC Sl 3 sts to cn and hold to back, k3,
k3 from cn.
6-st LC Sl 3 sts to cn and hold to front, k3,
k3 from cn.

CELLULAR STITCH

(over a multiple of 3 sts)
Rnd 1 Knit.
Rnd 2 *K2tog, yo, k1; rep from * around.
Rnd 3 Knit.
Rnd 4 *Yo, k1, k2tog; rep from * around.
Rep rnds 1–4 for cellular stitch

LEFT-SLANTING CABLE STRIP

(over a multiple of 6 sts)
Rnd 1 Purl.
Rnds 2–5 Knit.
Cable rnd 6 *Work 6-st LC; rep from *
around.
Rnd 7 Knit.

RIGHT-SLANTING CABLE STRIP

(over a multiple of 6 sts)
Rnd 1 Purl.
Rnds 2–5 Knit.
Cable rnd 6 *Work 6-st RC; rep from *
around.
Rnd 7 Knit.

COWL

Note For easier counting of this large
number of sts, pm on needle at intervals
while casting on.
With A, cast on 252 sts. Join to work in
rnds, taking care not to twist sts, and pm
to mark beg of rnd.

Section 1
LEFT-SLANTING CABLE STRIP
Note Beg with rnd 2 of left-slanting cable
for section 1 only.
With A, work rnds 2–7 of left-slanting
cable strip. Cut A.

FIRST CELLULAR STITCH BAND

Rnd 1 With B, purl.
Rnds 2–13 Work the cellular stitch for 3
reps of the 4-rnd pat.
Rnds 14 and 15 Knit. Cut B.
RIGHT-SLANTING CABLE STRIP
With A, work rnds 1–7 of right-slanting
cable strip. Cut A.
SECOND CELLULAR STITCH BAND
With B, work same as rnds 1–15 of first
cellular stitch band. Cut B.

Section 2
Worked over 28 rnds as foll:
With A, work rnds 1–7 of left-slanting cable
strip. Cut A. With B, work rnds 1–7 of right-
slanting cable strip. Cut B. With A, work rnds
1–7 of left-slanting cable strip. Cut A. With
B, work rnds 1–7 of right-slanting cable
strip. Cut B.

Section 3
With A, work rnds 1–15 of first cellular
stitch band. Cut A. With B, work rnds 1–7
of left-slanting cable strip. Cut B.

Section 4
With A, cont to work with decreased
shaping as foll:
Rnd 1 Purl.
Dec rnd 2 [K2, k2tog] 63 times—189 sts.
Rnds 3–5 Work rnds 2–4 of cellular stitch.
Dec rnd 6 [K1, k2tog] 63 times—126 sts.
Rnds 7–9 Work rnds 2–4 of cellular stitch.
Rnds 10–13 Work rnds 1–4 of cellular stitch.
Rnds 14 and 15 With A, knit. Cut A.

LAST SLANTING CABLE STRIP

With B, work rnds 1–7 of right-slanting
cable strip. Bind off.

FINISHING

Weave in ends on the WS. ✣

silver and gold

Make friends with this adorable cowl that showcases a favorite poem while keeping you warm and stylish.

silver and gold

■■■□

WHAT YOU NEED

Yarn
Tosh Sport **by Madelinetosh, 3½oz/100g hanks, each approx 270yd/246m (superwash merino wool)** (2)
• **1 hank in worn denim (A)**
Chickadee **by Quince & Co, 2½oz/73g skeins, each approx 181yd/166m (American wool)** (2)
• **1 hank in egret (B)**

Needles
• **One each size 4 (3.5mm) circular needles, 16"/40cm and 20"/50cm long** or size to obtain gauge

Notions
• **2 stitch markers**
• **Tapestry needle**

POEM COWL

Using words in art and design has been practiced throughout the ages. So why not knit a saying into a cowl? Easy charting and coordinating colors bring to life a favorite Girl Scout poem:

> **Make new friends**
> **But keep the old**
> **One is silver**
> **The other gold**

FINISHED MEASUREMENTS

Circumference (at lower edge) 22"/56cm
                  (at top edge) 17"/43cm
Height 12½"/32cm

GAUGES

22 sts and 40 rnds = 4"/10cm over seed st using size 4 (3.5mm) needle.
24 sts and 30 rnds = 4"/10cm over St st and chart pats using size 4 (3.5mm) needle.
Take time to check gauges.

SEED STITCH

(over an odd number of sts)
Rnd 1 K1, *p1, k1; rep from * around.
Rnd 2 P1, *k1, p1; rep from * around.
Rep rnds 1 and 2 for seed st.

K1, P1 RIB

(over an even number of sts)
Rnd 1 *K1, p1; rep from * around.
Rep rnd 1 for k1, p1 rib.

NOTE

When working the lettered color pat foll chart, bring new color up from under the working color and twist yarn to prevent holes in work. Carry the colors loosely across the WS of work. Also, cut color B at end of each color rnd and reattach B when beg the letter chart on the following rnd.

COWL

With A, cast on 121 sts. Join to work in rnds, taking care not to twist sts, and pm to mark beg of rnd. Work in seed st for 4"/10cm.
Knit 3 rnds with A.

BEGIN CHART 1

Set-up rnd Knit to end of rnd, remove marker, k26, place new marker. The newly placed marker will now be the beg of rnd marker and will also set up the chart placements.
Rnd 1 Work across all 62 sts of chart 1, then cut B (leaving a long end for weaving in later). K to end with A.
Rnds 2–6 Work as for rnd 1, foll chart 1.
Rows 7 and 8 With A, knit.

BEGIN CHART 2

Set-up rnd Remove marker, k6, place new marker, k to new marker. This sets up the placement of the chart 2 phrase in this new position.
Rnd 1 Beg chart 2 and work across all 56 sts of chart, cut B (leaving a long end for weaving in later), k to end with A.
Rnds 2–6 Work as for rnd 1 foll chart 2.
Rnds 7 and 8 With A, knit.

BEGIN CHART 3

Set-up rnd Remove marker, k6, place new marker, k to end. This sets up the placement of the chart 3 phrase in this new position.
Rnd 1 Beg chart 3 and work across all 68 sts of chart, cut B (leaving a long end for weaving in later), k to end with A.
Rnds 2–6 Work as for rnd 1 foll chart 3.
Rnds 7 and 8 With A, knit.

BEGIN CHART 4

Set-up rnd Remove marker, k6, place new marker, k to end. This sets up the placement of the chart 4 phrase in this new position.
Rnd 1 Beg chart 4 and work across all 75 sts of chart, cut B (leaving a long end for weaving in later), k to end with A.
Rnds 2–6 Work as for rnd 1 foll chart 4.
Rnds 7 and 8 With A, knit.
Rnds 9–12 Work in seed st with A.
Rnd 13 K2tog, *p1, k1; rep from * around, end p1—120 sts.
Cont in k1, p1 rib for a total of 3"/7.5cm in rib. Bind off in pat.

FINISHING

Weave in ends on the WS. Block lightly to measurements. ♣

Chart 4

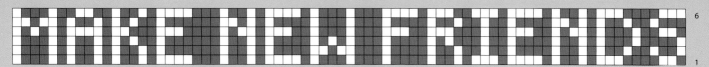

MAKE NEW FRIENDS

6

1

75 sts

Chart 3

BUT KEEP THE OLD

6

1

68 sts

Chart 2

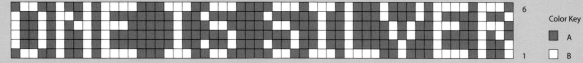

ONE IS SILVER

6

1

56 sts

Color Key

■ A
□ B

Chart 1

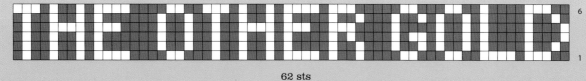

THE OTHER GOLD

6

1

62 sts

disco dreams

Can't stop, won't stop, don't stop the music.
Channel your inner disco diva in this paillette-trimmed collar.

disco dreams

■■■□

WHAT YOU NEED

Yarn
Cashmerino Aran **by Debbie Bliss/KFI,
1¾oz/50g balls, each approx 98yd/90m
(wool/acrylic/cashmere)** (4)
• **2 balls in #004 navy**

Needles
• **One each size 7 (4.5mm) circular
needles, 16"/40cm and 24"/60cm long** or
size to obtain gauge

Notions
• **4 stitch markers**
• **Tapestry needle**
• **3 packages (100 count in a package)
of 20mm large hole paillettes in
black (source: Cartwrights Sequins,
cartwright.com)**

PAILLETTES & RIBS COLLAR

I love sequins. Always shiny and playful,
the bigger, the better! Large black paillettes
are paired here with a stylish ribbed
collar in classic navy. Imagine other
combinations of bouncy, metallic sequins
with lighter yarns, each pairing making a
bold statement. Have fun!

FINISHED MEASUREMENTS

Circumference (around neck) 16"/40.5cm
Height (with turtleneck folded down)
7½"/19cm

GAUGE

20 sts and 30 rnds = 4"/10cm over k2, p2
rib, slightly stretched, using size 7 needles.
Take time to check gauge.

NOTE

First, use a tapestry needle to string all the
paillettes onto one ball of yarn so that they
are in place to begin working the paillette
rnds.

K2, P2 RIB

(over a multiple of 4 sts)
Rnd 1 *K2, p2; rep from * around.
Rep rnd 1 for k2, p2 rib.

Stitch Glossary

K1P (Knit 1 paillette) Bring yarn to front,
pull up one paillette on yarn and hold close
to RH needle, bring yarn to back, pull loop
knitwise through st below next st on LH
needle, k next st on LH needle, pass the
loop pulled from row below over st and off
needle to secure the paillette.

COLLAR

Cast on 156 sts using the ball with
stranded paillettes. Join, taking care not to
twist sts, and pm to mark beg of rnd.
Rnd 1 *K1, p1; rep from * around.
Rnd 2 Rep rnd 1.
Paillette rnd 3 *K1P, p1; rep from *
around.
Rnd 4 Knit.
Dec rnd 5 [K11, k2tog] 12 times—144 sts.
Paillette rnd 6 *K1, K1P; rep from *
around.
Rnd 7 Knit.
Dec rnd 8 [K10, k2tog] 12 times—132 sts.
Paillette rnd 9 *K1P, k1; rep from *
around.
Rnd 10 Knit.
Dec rnd 11 [K9, k2tog] 12 times—120 sts.
Paillette rnd 12 *K1, K1P; rep from *
around.
Rnd 13 Knit.
Change to shorter circular needle.
Dec rnd 14 *K1, k2tog tbl; rep from *
around—80 sts.
Rnd 15 Knit.

Begin turtleneck
Cont in rnds of k2, p2 rib for 9"/23cm. Bind
off in rib.

FINISHING

Weave in ends on the WS.❖

all seasons

For year-round fiber wear, linen is always a winner.
Wear this striped and drapey cowl long or doubled up.

all seasons

■■■■

WHAT YOU NEED

Yarn

Kestrel **by Quince & Co**, 1¾oz/50g **skeins, each approx 76yd/70m (linen)** (**4**)
- **4 skeins in #500 senza (A)**
- **1 skein each in #506 rosehip (B), #504 pebble (C), #507 yarrow (D), and #505 urchin (E)**

Needles
- **One pair size 9 (5.5mm) needles** or size to obtain gauge
- **One extra size 9 (5.5mm) needle for 3-needle bind-off**

Notions
- **Stitch marker**
- **Tapestry needle**

STRIPED COWL

Linen has qualities that makes it perfect for any occasion and season. The weight is light enough for summer, but bold enough to challenge colder weather. When blocked, the drape and feel are even more luxurious than when it is on the needles. It's truly a yarn for all seasons.

FINISHED MEASUREMENTS

Width 13½"/34cm
Length 52"/132cm
Note The hang of the scarf, worn without wrapping around the neck, is 26"/66cm.

GAUGE

18 sts and 26 rows = 4"/10cm over St st, after blocking, using size 9 (5.5mm) needles.
Take time to check gauge.

RIDGE PATTERN

(work with A over any number of sts)
Row 1 (RS) Sl 1, k3, p to the last 4 sts, k4.
Row 2 (WS) Sl 1, k to end.
Row 3 Rep row 2.
Row 4 Rep row 1.
Rows 5 and 6 Rep row 2.
Rows 7 and 8 Rep row 1.
Row 9 Rep row 2.
Rows 10 and 11 Rep row 1.
Row 12 Rep row 2.
These 12 rows form the ridge pat.

COWL

With A, cast on 60 sts.

First Half
Row 1 (RS) Sl 1, k to end.
Row 2 (WS) Sl 1, k3, p to last 4 sts, k4.
Rows 3–6 Rep rows 1 and 2 twice more.
Rows 7–18 Work rows 1–12 of ridge pat.
Rows 19–28 Rep rows 1 and 2 five times more. Cut A.
STRIPE 1
Row 1 (RS) With B, Sl 1, k to end.
Rows 1–26 With B, rep rows 1 and 2 thirteen times more. Cut B.
STRIPE 2
Rows 1–12 With A, rep rows 1 and 2 six times more. Cut A.
STRIPE 3
Rows 1–26 With C, rep rows 1 and 2 thirteen times more. Cut C.
STRIPE 4
Rep stripe 2.
STRIPE 5
Rows 1–26 With D, rep rows 1 and 2 thirteen times more. Cut D.

STRIPE 6
Rep stripe 2.
STRIPE 7
Rows 1–26 With E, rep rows 1 and 2 thirteen times more. Cut E.
STRIPE 8
Rep stripe 2, but do not cut A.

Second Half
Note The rem of the cowl is worked with A only. Rows 1 and 2 of first half be referred to for segments in St st between the ridge pat segments in this half.
Rows 1–12 Work rows 1–12 of ridge pat (for 3 ridges).
Next 18 rows Rep rows 1 and 2 nine times more.
Next 22 rows Work rows 1–12 of ridge pat once, then rows 3–12 once more (for 5 ridges).
Next 20 rows Rep rows 1 and 2 ten times more.
Next 8 rows Work rows 1–8 of ridge pat once (for 2 ridges).
Next 20 rows Rep rows 1 and 2 ten times more.
Next 22 rows Work rows 1–12 of ridge pat once, then rows 3–12 once more (for 5 ridges).
Next 18 rows Rep rows 1 and 2 nine times more. Leave sts on needle.

FINISHING

With A, pick up and k 60 sts from the RS of the cast-on edge. Then with RS of the cast-on edge sts and the last row of cowl sts tog and with the needle points facing the same direction, join the 2 edges tog using 3-needle bind-off method (see page 141). Weave in ends on the WS. Block finished piece using wet block and steam iron method.❖

brave new world

Look to the plains of the American West and you'll find the sandwashed
desert hues and patterns that play out on this double-faced cowl.

brave new world

■■■□

WHAT YOU NEED

Yarn
- Washable Wool Collection, DK weight **by Swan's Island, 1¾oz/50g skeins, each approx 140yd/128m (merino wool)** 🄳
- **2 skeins each in #216 mushroom (A) and in #210 verdigris (B)**

Needles
- **One size 6 (4mm) circular needle, 16"/40cm long** or size to obtain gauge

Notions
- **3 stitch markers**
- **Tapestry needle**

PATTERNS COWL

Using a classic shape, this cowl is a creative spin on Fair Isle patterning. With just two colors and doubled-up yarn for texture, multiple patterns are created. In soft, stitch-defining yarn, it's a bold new way to showcase the traditional essence of Fair Isle!

FINISHED MEASUREMENTS

Circumference 22"/56cm
Height 8"/20.5cm

GAUGE

21 sts and 32 rnds = 4"/10cm over St st foll charts and ridge pat using size 6 (4mm) needle.
Take time to check gauge.

NOTES

1) Cowl is worked in rounds for a doubled fabric thickness with the join of each rnd hidden and facing the inside. It is not necessary, therefore, to adjust the staggered color that occurs at the join.
2) Every ridge rnd is worked with 1 strand of A & B held tog as a purl rnd.

COWL

With A, cast on 84 sts. Join to work in rnds, taking care not to twist sts, and pm to mark beg of rnd.

Rnd 1 With A, knit.
Ridge rnd 2 With A & B held tog, purl.
Rnd 3 With B, knit.

Begin Chart 1
Rnds 4 and 5 Work the 4-st rep of chart 1 for 2 rnds.
Rnds 6 and 7 With A, knit.
Ridge rnd 8 Rep ridge rnd 2.
Rnds 9 and 10 With A, knit.
Rnds 11 and 12 With B, knit.
Rnds 13–16 Rep rnds 9–12.
Rnds 17 and 18 With A, knit.
Ridge rnd 19 Rep ridge rnd 2.
Rnd 20 With B, knit.

Begin Chart 2
Rnds 21–23 Work the 4-st rep of chart 2 for 3 rnds.
Rnds 24 and 25 With B, knit.
Ridge rnd 26 Rep ridge rnd 2.
Rnds 27 and 28 With A, knit.
Ridge rnd 29 Rep ridge rnd 2.
Rnds 30 and 31 With A, knit.
Rnds 32–37 With B, knit.
Rnds 38 and 39 With A, knit.
Ridge rnd 40 Rep ridge rnd 2.
Rnds 41 and 42 With A, knit.

Begin Chart 3
Rnds 43–45 Work the 4-st rep of chart 3 for 3 rnds.
Rnds 46 and 47 With A, knit.
Ridge rnd 48 Rep ridge rnd 2.
Rnds 49–51 With B, knit.

Begin Chart 4
Rnds 52–54 Work the 4-st rep of chart 4 for 3 rnds
Rnds 55 and 56 With A, knit.
Ridge rnd 57 Rep ridge rnd 2.
Rnds 58 and 59 With B, knit.
Ridge rnd 60 Rep ridge rnd 2.
Rnds 61 and 62 With A, knit.
Ridge rnd 63 Rep ridge rnd 2.
Rnd 64 With A, knit.

Begin Chart 5
Rnds 65–68 Work the 4-st rep of chart 5 for 4 rnds.
Rnd 69 With B, knit.
Ridge rnd 70 Rep ridge rnd 2.

Rnds 71–75 With A, knit.
Ridge rnd 76 Rep ridge rnd 2.
Rnd 77 With B, knit.

Begin Chart 1
Rnds 78–85 Work the 4-st rep of chart 1 for 8 rnds.
Ridge rnd 86 Rep ridge rnd 2.
Rnds 87 and 88 With B, knit.
Rnds 89–94 With A, knit.
Rnds 95–97 With B, knit.
Rnds 98–104 Rep rnds 57–63.
Rnds 105 and 106 With B, knit.

Begin Chart 6
Rnds 107–112 Work the 4-st rep of chart 6 for 6 rnds.
Rnds 113 and 114 With A, knit.
Ridge rnd 115 Rep ridge rnd 2.
Rnds 116–120 With A, knit.
Rnds 121–126 With B, knit.
Ridge rnd 127 Rep ridge rnd 2.
Rnds 128 and 129 With B, knit.

Begin Chart 7
Rnds 130–132 Work the 4-st rep of chart 7 for 3 rnds.
Rnds 133 and 134 With B, knit.
Ridge rnd 135 Rep ridge rnd 2.
Rnds 136 and 137 With A, knit.
Ridge rnd 138 Rep ridge rnd 2.
Rnds 139 and 140 With B, knit.

Begin Chart 1
Rnds 141 and 142 Work the 4-st rep of chart 1 for 2 rnds.
Rnd 143 With A, knit.
Ridge rnd 144 Rep ridge rnd 2.
Rnds 145 and 146 With A, knit.
Rnds 147 and 148 With B, knit.
Rnds 149–156 Rep rnds 145–148 two times more.
Ridge rnd 157 Rep ridge rnd 2.
Rnds 158 and 159 With B, knit.
Ridge rnd 160 Rep ridge rnd 2.
Rnds 161 and 162 With A, knit.

Begin Chart 5
Rnds 163–166 Work the 4-st rep of chart 5 for 4 rnds.
Rnds 167 and 168 With B, knit.
Ridge rnd 169 Rep ridge rnd 2.

Rnds 170 and 171 With B, knit.
Bind off knitwise.

FINISHING
Weave in ends on the WS. Sew the cast-on
edge and bind-off edge tog forming the
doubled fabric tube. Then, with the joining
at the inside center, lightly block the cowl
flat.❖

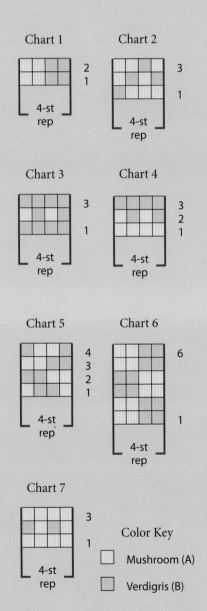

Chart 1

2
1

4-st
rep

Chart 2

3

1

4-st
rep

Chart 3

3

1

4-st
rep

Chart 4

3
2
1

4-st
rep

Chart 5

4
3
2
1

4-st
rep

Chart 6

6

1

4-st
rep

Chart 7

3

1

4-st
rep

Color Key

☐ Mushroom (A)

▨ Verdigris (B)

puff piece

Cool shades of blue and green are punctuated by a shock of bright yellow in this crisply striped neck piece with a split polo collar.

puff piece

■■■□

WHAT YOU NEED

Yarn

Puffin **by Quince & Co,** 3½oz/100g **hanks, each approx 112yd/102m (wool)** ⬛
- **1 hank in each in peacock (A), carrie's yellow (B), belize (C), glacier (D), and pea coat (E)**

Needles
- **One each size 10½ (6.5mm) circular needles, 16"/40cm and 24"/60cm long** or size to obtain gauge

Notions
- **3 stitch markers**
- **Tapestry needle**

POLO PUFFIN COLLAR

Three sections make up this cowl-collar: the ribbed polo collar, the turtleneck, and the shoulder section. Starting from the top and worked downward, the structure lends itself well to vibrant striping. A snug fit makes this handsome piece a warm choice for even the coldest days.

FINISHED MEASUREMENTS

Shoulder circumference 32"/81cm
Neck circumference 17"/43cm
Height (with collar unfolded) 14½"/37cm
Height (with collar folded) 9"/23cm

GAUGE

15 sts and 22 rnds = 4"/10cm over k2, p1 rib, slightly stretched, using size 10½ (6.5mm) needle.
Take time to check gauge.

NOTE

When changing to a new color in the stripe pat while working in the rib pats, the first row or rnd will be worked as knit for a crisp line at the color stripe change.

K2, P1 RIB

(worked in rnds over a multiple of 3 sts)
Rnd 1 *K2, p1; rep from * around.
Rep rnd 1 for k2, p1 rib.

COWL

Collar

Beg at the top (neck) edge of the cowl, with larger circular needle and A, cast on 86 sts. Work back and forth in rows as foll:
Row 1 (RS) K2, *p2, k2; rep from * to end.
Row 2 (WS) P2, *k2, p2; rep from * to end.
Rows 3–6 Rep rows 1 and 2 twice more. Cut A.
Row 7 (RS) With B, knit.
Row 8 Rep row 2.
Rows 9–10 Rep rows 1 and 2. Cut B.
Rows 11–14 With C, rep rows 7–10. Cut C.
Row 15 (RS) With A, knit.
Row 16 Repeat row 2.
Rows 17–24 Repeat rows 1 and 2 four times more.
Dec row 25 (RS) With A, k2tog, *p2, k2tog; rep from * to end—64 sts.
This ends the collar. At this point, the piece will be joined to work rem of cowl in rnds as foll:
Joining rnd Bring the 2 needle points tog as for working in rnds and turn the work to the WS; sl the last st on the RH needle back to LH needle and pm in this new position on the RH needle; then bring A yarn to front and p the first 2 sts tog; then cont in k2, p1 rib around—63 sts.
Rnds 1–5 With A, work in p1, k2 rib. Cut A.
Rnd 6 With D, knit.
Rnds 7–13 With D, work p1, k2 rib. Cut D.
Rnd 14 With E, knit.
Rnds 15–22 With E, work in p1, k2 rib. Cut E.

Beg Shoulder Increases

Set-up rnd 23 With B, [k21, pm] twice, k21.
Rnd 24 With B, work in p1, k2 rib.
Inc rnd 25 With B, *p1, M1, work in established rib to marker, M1, sl marker; rep from * twice more—6 sts inc'd.
Rnd 26 With B, working the M1 st into the rib pat, work in p1, k2 rib retaining the p1 sts at each side of the markers.
Rnds 27–30 Rep inc rnd 25 and rnd 26 twice more.
Rnd 31 Rep inc rnd 25—87 sts. Cut B.
Rnd 32 With A, knit.
Inc rnd 33 Rep inc rnd 25.
Rnd 34 Rep rnd 26.
Rnd 35 Rep inc rnd 33—99 sts. Cut A.
Rnd 36 With D, knit.
Inc rnd 37 Rep inc rnd 25.
Rnd 38 Rep rnd 26.
Rnds 39 and 40 Rep rnds 37 and 38—111 sts. Cut D.
Rnd 41 With C, knit.
Rnd 42 Rep inc rnd 25.
Rnd 43 Rep rnd 26.
Rnds 44 and 45 Rep rnds 42 and 43—123 sts. Bind off in rib.

FINISHING

Do not block or steam the finished piece. Weave in ends on the WS.✤

bold shoulder

Catch fire in this quick-to-knit oversized cowl
that uses multiple show-off stitches in a bulky yarn.

bold shoulder

■■■□

WHAT YOU NEED
Yarn
Magnum **by Cascade Yarns, 8.82oz/250g skeins, each approx 123yd/112m (wool)** (6)
• **2 skeins in #9465B burnt orange**

Needles
• **One size 13 (9mm) circular needle, 32"/80cm long** or size to obtain gauge

Notions
• **Stitch marker**
• **Tapestry needle**

LOOPY COWL
There's nothing like a robust cowl worked up in bulky wool to battle a cold day. To bounce up the texture, multiple boisterous stitch patterns are used: bobbles, dropped stitches, and loops. It's a "noisy" but joyous sampler.

FINISHED MEASUREMENTS
Circumference 45½"/115.5cm
Height 14"/35.5cm

GAUGE
7 sts and 14 rnds = 4"/10cm over seed st pat using size 13 (9mm) needle.
Take time to check gauge.

SEED STITCH
(worked in rnds over an even number of sts)
Rnd 1 *K1, p1; rep from * around.
Rnd 2 *P1, k1; rep from * around.
Rep rnds 1 and 2 for seed st.

STITCH GLOSSARY
KW3 (Knit wrapping 3 times) Knit st, wrapping yarn 3 times around needle before slipping st from LH needle.
MB6 (Make 6-st bobble) [K into front and back of st] 3 times, then with LH needle, pull the first 5 sts over the last st, then k final st.
K-loop (Knit loop) To create an extended loop in each st, work as foll: *knit into a st, place new loop on RH needle but do not let the st on LH needle drop from needle yet; then bring the working yarn to front and wrap around your LH thumb and pull yarn out to measure approx 1"/2.5cm loop; bring working yarn to the back and k the st on LH needle and pull the "new" st on the RH needle over it, fastening in place the loop; rep from * for each k-loop st around.

COWL
Cast on 80 sts. Join, taking care not to twist sts, and pm to mark beg of rnd.
Rnds 1–14 Work in seed st.
Rnd 15 Purl.
Rnd 16 KW3 in each st around.
Rnd 17 Slip each st around (without knitting), dropping the extra loops in each st.
Rnd 18 Knit.
Rnd 19 Purl.
Rnds 20 and 21 Knit.
Rnd 22 *K3, MB6; rep from * nineteen times more.
Rnd 23 *K3, k1tbl; rep from * around.
Rnd 24 Knit.
Rnd 25 Purl.
Rnd 26 Knit.
Loop rnd 27 Work k-loop in each st around.
Rnd 28 Knit.
Loop rnd 29 Work k-loop in each st around.
Rnd 30 Knit.
Rnd 31 Purl.
Rnd 32 Knit.
Rnd 33 KW3 in each st around.
Rnd 34 Slip each st around (without knitting), dropping the extra loops in each st.
Rnd 35 Knit.
Rnd 36 Purl.
Rnd 37–45 Work in seed st.
Bind off in seed st pat.

FINISHING
Weave in ends on the WS.✤

electric avenue

Staid, bookish tweed gets a shot of high voltage from bright chartreuse
trimming in this zigzag supersized cowl.

electric avenue

■■□□

WHAT YOU NEED

Yarn

ASAP **by Madelinetosh, 4½oz/127g skeins, each approx 90yd/82m (merino wool)** (6)
- **2 skeins in grasshopper (A)**
- **1 skein in optic (B)**

Needles
- **One size 13 (9mm) circular needle, 24"/60cm long** or size to obtain gauge

Notions
- **Stitch markers**
- **Tapestry needlee**

ZIGZAG COWL

I love the dynamic quality of the spiral stitch in this cowl. It's easy to knit and feels like it has inherent movement. To add to that feeling, mix a printed yarn with a bright, solid border. You'll have a cowl that's full of bold contrasts and interest.

FINISHED MEASUREMENTS

Circumference 28"/71cm
Depth 19"/48cm

GAUGE

10 sts and 14 rnds = 4"/10cm over St st or diagonal pattern stitch using size 13 (9mm) needle.
Take time to check gauge.

STITCH GLOSSARY

Kfb K into front and back of st—1 st increased.

COWL

With A, cast on 70 sts. Join to work in rnds, taking care not to twist sts, and pm to mark beg of rnd.

BEGIN CHART PATTERN

Rnd 1 With A, *k5, p5; rep from * around.
Rnd 2 With A, *p1, k5, p4; rep from * around.
Cont with A, working chart as established, through rnd 10, then rep rnds 1–10 twice more.
Cut A.
Next rnd With B, knit.
Note The zigzag pattern will now slant in the opposite direction (see rnds 11–20 of chart).
Cont to work rnds 11–20 of chart with B until these 10 rnds have been worked 3 times, ending with a chart rnd 20.
Cut B.
Next rnd With A, knit.
Note The zigzag pattern will now slant in the opposite direction (see rnds 1–10 of chart).
Cont to work rnds 1–10 of chart with A until piece measures 19"/48cm from beg.
Bind off in pat.

FINISHING

Weave in ends on the WS.❖

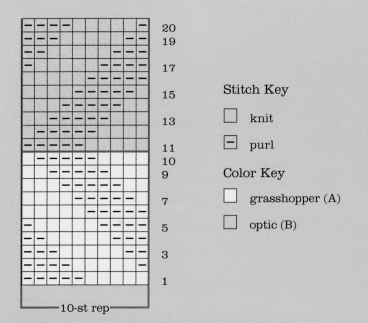

Stitch Key

□ knit

⊟ purl

Color Key

□ grasshopper (A)

□ optic (B)

10-st rep

carousel confection

Remember the fun of the midway with bright beads that trace the ripples
of this otherwise serious grey, black, and white high neck cowl.

carousel confection

■■■□

WHAT YOU NEED

Yarn
Rios **by Malabrigo, 3½oz/100g skeins, each approx 210yd/193m (wool)** (🄳)
• 1 skein each in #RIO195 black (A), #RIO043 plomo (B), and #RIO063 natural (C)

Needles
• One size 6 (4mm) circular needle, 20"/50cm long or size to obtain gauge

Notions
• Stitch marker
• Tapestry needle
• 390 small/mini multicolor pony beads (4mm x 7mm)

BEADED COWL

I love pony beads for knitting because they're bright, affordable, and won't weigh down or stretch out the fabric. They are added here in the cast-on round using the long-tail method. It takes patience and counting to establish the border, but the end result is eye-catching fun!

FINISHED MEASUREMENTS

Circumference 20"/51cm
Height 11½"/29cm

GAUGE

26 sts and 30 rnds = 4"/10cm over fairground ripple pattern using size 6 (4mm) needle.
Take time to check gauge.

FAIRGROUND RIPPLE PATTERN

(over a multiple of 13 sts)
Rnd 1 *Ssk, k9, k2tog; rep from * around.
Rnd 2 Knit.
Rnd 3 *Ssk, k7, k2tog; rep from * around.
Rnd 4 Knit.
Rnd 5 *Ssk, [yo, k1] 5 times, yo, k2tog; rep from * around.
Rnd 6 Purl.
Work these 6 rnds for fairground ripple pat worked in alternating color bands as indicated in the instructions for the cowl.

K1, P1 RIB

(over a multiple of 2 sts)
Rnd 1 *K1, p1; rep from * around.
Rep rnd 1 for k1, p1 rib.

BEAD APPLICATION

The beads are incorporated into the cast-on edge in color A and then into rnd 1 of the pat when first using colors B and C. First, using the tapestry needle, thread 130 beads onto the ball in color A, then 130 beads onto each ball in colors B and C.

COWL

With A (with the stranded beads on the end), measure an approx 4yd/3.75m length of yarn from the end for a long tail cast-on and place a slipknot at this point. Cast on 1 st, *slide the bead up against the needle before looping the yarn around the thumb to cast on the next st, cast on 1 st; rep from * until all beads are in place and 130 sts have been cast on. Join to work in rnds, taking care not to twist sts, and pm to mark beg of rnd.
Set-up rnd With A, knit.
Then, cont with A, work rnds 1–6 of the fairground ripple pattern. Cut A.
Bead rnd With color B, *k1, slide one bead up against the needle; rep from * around.
Set-up rnd With B, knit.
Then, cont with B, work rnds 1–6 of the fairground ripple pattern. Cut B.
Bead rnd With color C, *k1, slide one bead up against the needle; rep from * around.
Set-up rnd With C, knit.
Then, cont with C, work rnds 1–6 of the fairground ripple pattern. Cut C.
The beads are now all in place.
Rnd 1 With A, knit.
Rnds 2–7 With A, work rnds 1–6 of fairground ripple pattern. Cut A.
Rnds 8–14 With B, rep rnds 1–7. Cut B.
Rnds 15–21 With C, rep rnds 1–7. Cut C.
Rep rnds 1–21 twice more, then rnds 1–7 once more.
Rnd 1 With B, knit.
Rnd 2 *K1, p1; rep from * around.
Rnds 3–6 Rep rnd 2.
Bind off in rib.

FINISHING

Weave in ends on the WS.✤

poncho v

Turn heads with the lovely drape and deep cowl neck
of this uniquely constructed poncho.

poncho v

■■□□

WHAT YOU NEED

Yarn
Chunky **by Misti Alpaca, 3½oz/100g
hanks, each approx 109yd/100m
(baby alpaca)** ⓑ
• **6 hanks in #RJ1662 samba**

Needles
• **One size 10 (6mm) circular needle,
29"/74cm long** or size to obtain gauge
• **One size 10 (6mm) extra needle
for working the 3-needle bind-off**

Notions
• **Stitch marker**
• **Tapestry needle**

CHUNKY PONCHO

This is the simplest of poncho shapes—
a scarf folded end-to-end, with a cowl
extension. The all-over checkerboard stitch
pattern complements the minimalism of
the design while adding texture.

FINISHED MEASUREMENTS
Lower edge 52"/132cm
Depth to shoulder 10½"/26.5cm
Neck circumference 25"/63.5cm

GAUGE
16 sts and 23 rows = 4"/10cm over
checkerboard pat st using size 10 (6mm)
needle. **Take time to check gauge.**

CHECKERBOARD PATTERN STITCH
(worked in rows over a multiple of 10 sts).
Row 1 (RS) *K5, p5; rep from * to end.
Rows 2–6 Rep row 1.
Row 7 (RS) *P5, k5; rep from * to end.
Rows 8–12 Rep row 7.
Rep rows 1–12 for checkerboard pat st
worked in rows.

CHECKERBOARD PATTERN STITCH
(worked in rnds over a multiple of 10 sts).
Rnds 1–6 *K5, p5; rep from * around.
Rnds 7–12 *P5, k5; rep from * around.
Rep rnds 1–12 for checkerboard pat st
worked in rnds.

PONCHO
Cast on 200 sts.
Working the checkerboard pat st worked in
rows, work the 12-row pat rep for 5 reps.
Piece measures approx 10½"/26.5cm from beg.

PRE-FINISHING
Note For instructions on how to work the
3-needle bind-off, see page 141.
To finish the one shoulder edge and to form
the set-up for the cowl collar, first fold the
just knit piece in half at the center with the
right sides of the piece tog. Then using the
spare needle from the WS of work, work a
3-needle bind-off to join the first 50 sts to
the last 50 sts of the row (see schematic).
Flip the work so that the rem 100 sts are in
place to be worked in rnds from the RS.
Beg the cowl
With the attached yarn and working the
checkerboard pat st worked in rnds, work
rnd 1 of checkerboard pat st, and pm at
end, then join to work in rnds. Cont in
checkerboard pat worked in rnds for 7 reps
of the 12-rnd pat. Bind off in pat.

FINISHING
Weave in ends on the WS.❖

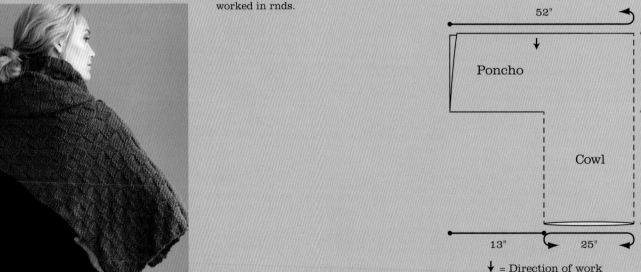

52"

Poncho

10½

13"   25"

Cowl

15"

↓ = Direction of work

— = Indicates 3-Needle Bind-Off

tiny bobbles

Bobbles, bobbles, and more bobbles! Add some whimsy to your life
with this playful cowl that's knit from elastic-blend yarn.
Pick your own color combinations for extra fun!

tiny bobbles

■■■□

WHAT YOU NEED

Yarn
Fixation **by Cascade Yarns, 1¾oz/50g hanks, each approx 100yd/91m (cotton/elastic)** ⓷
• **3 hanks in #7625 fawn (A)**
• **1 hank each in #8176 ecru (B), #8418 silver (C), #8990 black (D), #2625 blueberry (E), #2608 denim (F), #7988 taupe (G), and #7382 chocolate (H)**

Needles
• **One size 7 (4.5mm) circular needle, 16"/40cm long** or size to obtain gauge

Notions
• **3 stitch markers**
• **Tapestry needle**

BOBBLE COWL

This cowl offers a fun challenge in its 748 bobbles! The densely textured fabric is soft and comfortable when worn close to the neck. The cotton/elastic yarn blend is easy on the hands, an important factor when manipulating yarn. Colors alternate to create a defined pattern. Or, knit the bobbles randomly for a different look.

FINISHED MEASUREMENTS

Circumference 23"/58.5cm
Height 8"/20.5cm

GAUGE

26 sts and 30 rnds = 4"/10cm over St st using size 7 (4.5mm) needles.
Take time to check gauge.

NOTE

The cowl is worked in a double layer with color A on the WS in St st (with reverse St st trims on each edge for the fold), then the bobble trimmed section on the RS worked on a background of St st in A. Color B bobble will be worked on every bobble rnd 3 with all the other colors alternated on bobble rnd 6, as desired.

STITCH GLOSSARY

MB (make bobble) With chosen contrast color (either B, C, D, E, F, G or H), [k into front and back of st] 3 times, then with LH needle, pull the first 5 sts over the last st, one at a time, then k final st.

COWL

With A, cast on 104 sts. Join to work in rnds, taking care not to twist sts, and pm to mark beg of rnd.
Rnd 1 K26, pm, p4, k44, p4, pm, k26.
Rnd 2 Rep rnd 1, slipping markers.
Bobble rnd 3 K26 with A, sl marker, p4 with A, *k3 with A, MB with B; rep from * 10 times more, p4 with A, sl marker, k26 with A.
Rnd 4 With A, rep rnd 1, knitting all the bobble sts tbl.
Rnd 5 With A, rep rnd 1.
Bobble rnd 6 K26 with A, sl marker, p4 with A, k1 with A, *MB with C (or desired color), k3 with A; rep from * 9 times more, MB with C (or desired color), k2 with A, p4 with A, sl marker, k26 with A.
Rnd 7 Rep rnd 4.
Rnd 8 Rep rnd 5.
Rep rows 3–8 (for 6-rnd rep) working each consecutive bobble rnd 6 in desired alternate color (C–H) for 34 times more. With A, bind off all sts knitwise.

FINISHING

Turn the tube to the WS and tie off all the ends and cut to 1"/2.5cm length. It is not necessary to weave the ends into the fabric as they will all fall to the inside of the cowl. Turn the tube to the RS. With tapestry needle, sew the bound-off edge to the cast-on edge using mattress st. Block very lightly to measurements. ❖

just fur fun

For night dazzle or day drama, new generations of sparkly faux fur yarns
are on display in this convertible hooded cowl.

just fur fun

∎∎∎◻

WHAT YOU NEED

Yarn

La Furla Metal **by Trendsetter Yarns,
3½oz/100g balls, each approx 65yd/60m
(polyamide/metallic/polyester)** (4)
For cowl only (for cowl plus hood)
• 1 (2) balls in #45 brown (A)
• 1 (2) balls in #110 smoke silver (B)
Duchess **by Trendsetter Yarns, 1¾oz/50g
balls, each approx 130yd/119m (wool/
cashmere/polyamide)** (4)
For cowl only (for cowl plus hood)
• 2 (3) balls in #304 charcoal (C)

Needles

• **One each sizes 8 and 10½ (5 and 6.5mm)
circular needles, each 24"/60cm long** or
size to obtain gauge
• **One extra size 10½ (6.5mm) needle for
3-needle bind-off**

Notions

• **Stitch marker**
• **Tapestry needle**

FUZZY CONVERTIBLE COWL

Knitting with faux fur requires different
techniques and approaches. You'll be able
to better see the texture if you knit it with
some space. Do this by inserting one or
two rows of regular yarn or doubling it
up with a regular yarn strand. Have fun
knitting this combination cowl/hood that's
remarkably warm!

FINISHED MEASUREMENTS

Circumference 30"/76cm
Height (without hood) 10"/25.5cm
         (with hood) 19"/48cm

GAUGES

15 sts and 18 rnds = 4"/10cm over St st
using smaller needle and alternating 1 rnd
of A or B with 1 rnd of C.
13 sts and 16 rows = 4"/10cm over St st
using larger needle and A and C held tog.
Take time to check gauges.

NOTE

The cowl is worked in rnds using the
smaller needle and alternating one rnd of
A or B with 1 rnd of C.
The hood is worked back and forth in rows
using the larger needle and A or B held tog
with C.

COWL

With smaller needle and C, cast on 112 sts.
Join to work in rnds, taking care not to
twist sts, and pm to mark beg of rnd.
Rnd 1 With C, knit.
Rnd 2 With C, purl.
Rnd 3 With A, knit.
Rnd 4 With C, purl.
Rnd 5 With B, knit.
Rnd 6 With C, purl.

Rep rnds 3–6 (for garter stripe pat worked
in rnds) until piece measures 6"/15cm from
beg, ending with a rnd worked in A or B
(fur yarn).
Dec rnd With C, [p9, p2tog] 10 times, end
p2—102 sts.
Cont in the 4-rnd garter stripe pat
as established until piece measures
10"/25.5cm from beg.
Note If you are making the cowl version,
bind off all sts and weave in ends on WS
at this point. To work the hooded version,
cont as foll:

Hood

Change to larger circular needle and work
back and forth in rows as foll:
Row 1 (RS) With B and C held tog, knit.
Row 2 (WS) Rep row 1.
Rows 3 and 4 With A and C held tog, knit.
Rep rows 1–4 for garter st (worked in
rows) until hood measures 4½"/11.5cm
from the beg of the opening. Then, cont in
St st as foll:
Row 1 (RS) With B and C held tog, knit.
Row 2 (WS) With B and C held tog, purl.
Row 3 With A and C held tog, knit.
Row 4 With A and C held tog, purl.
Rep these 2 rows for St st (worked in rows)
until hood measures 9"/23cm from the beg
of the hood opening.

FINISHING

Divide sts evenly between two needles with
points facing in the same direction. Using
3-needle bind-off method (see page 141),
join top of hood tog. Weave in ends on the
WS.❖

winter classic

When winter winds blow, escape into this toasty set
that uses the Fair Isle technique for extra warmth.

winter classic

■■■■

WHAT YOU NEED
Yarn
- Toboggan **by Classic Elite Yarns, 3½oz/100g hanks, each approx 87yd/80m (wool/alpaca)** 🄺
- **2 hanks each in #6716 natural (A), #6713 ebony (B), #6731 periwinkle (C), #6794 emerald (D), and #6780 laurel (E)**

Needles
Cowl
- **One size 10 (6mm) circular needle, 24"/60cm long** or size to obtain gauge
Hat
- **One size 10 (6mm) circular needle, 16"/40cm long** or size to obtain gauge
- **One set (4) size 10 (6mm) double-pointed needles (dpns)**

Notions
- **Stitch marker**
- **Tapestry needle**

FAIR ISLE COWL & HAT
Fair Isle patterns are a timeless classic. Vibrant colors and very soft yarn make this duo a must-have for cold winter days. The variety of colored textures might look complicated but because of the thick gauge, each section works up quickly.

FINISHED MEASUREMENTS
Cowl
- **Circumference** 24"/61cm
- **Height** 8½"/21.5cm
Hat
- **Circumference** 22"/56cm
- **Height** 9½"/24cm

GAUGE
13 sts and 18 rnds = 4"/10cm over St st and color charts using size 10 (6mm) needles.
Take time to check gauge.
Note When changing colors, bring new color up from under the working color and twist yarns to prevent holes in work. Carry the colors loosely across the WS of work.

COWL
Using colors A and B, *cast on 1 st with A, cast on 1 st with B; rep from * for a total of 70 sts. Join to work in rnds, taking care not to twist sts, and pm to mark beg of rnd.

Begin Rolled Two-Color Edge
Rnd 1 (WS) *K1 with A, k1 with B; rep from * around being sure to bring the new color up from under the previous color using a consistent tension. This stranding technique will appear on the RS when the edge rolls after completion.
Rnds 2–6 Rep rnd 1.
Turn work so that the WS and RS of work are reversed.
Rnd 7 (RS) K the A sts with A and the B sts with B.
Rnd 8 (RS) With B, [k6, kfb] 10 times—80 sts.
Rnd 9 With B, knit.

Begin Chart A
Work 6 rnds foll chart A, completing the 4-st rep twenty times each rnd.
Begin Chart B
Work 9 rnds foll chart B, completing the 8-st rep ten times each rnd.
Begin Chart C
Work 6 rnds foll chart C, completing the 4-st rep twenty times each rnd.
Then, work as foll:
Next rnd With E, knit.
Next inc rnd With E, [k7, kfb] 10 times—90 sts. Cut E.

Two-Color Rib
Rnd 1 *K1 with D, k1 with A; rep from * around.
Rnd 2 *K1 with D, p1 with A; rep from * around.
Rnds 3 and 4 Rep rnd 2.
Rnd 5 *K1 with B, p1 with A; rep from * around.
Rnd 6 Rep rnd 5.
Then, bind off all sts knitwise matching colors A and B and stranding as for the beg of the cowl.

FINISHING
Weave in ends on the WS.

HAT
Beg at the top edge with dpn and A, cast on 6 sts and divide sts evenly onto 3 needles with 2 sts on each needle. Join to work in rnds taking care not to twist sts on needles and pm to mark beg of rnd.
Rnd 1 With A, knit.
Rnd 2 With A, (kfb) 6 times—12 sts.
Rnd 3 With A, knit.
Rnd 4 With E, (kfb) 12 times—24 sts.
Rnd 5 With A, knit.
Rnd 6 With A, [k1, kfb] 12 times—36 sts.
Rnd 7 With E, knit.
Rnd 8 With E, [k2, kfb] 12 times—48 sts.
Rnd 9 With A, knit.
Rnd 10 With A, [k3, kfb] 12 times—60 sts.
Rnd 11 With E, knit.
Rnd 12 With E, [k4, kfb] 12 times—72 sts.
Rnd 13 With A, knit.
Change to circular needle.
Turning rnd 14 With 1 strand of A and B held tog, purl.
Rnd 15 With B, knit.

Begin Chart A
Work 6 rnds foll chart A, completing the 4-st rep twenty times each rnd.
Begin Chart B
Work 9 rnds foll chart B, completing the 8-st rep ten times each rnd.
Begin Chart C
Work 6 rnds foll chart C, completing the 4-st rep twenty times each rnd.

Brim
Using a double strand of yarn on the purl rnds, work the brim in garter st as foll:
Rnd 1 With A and D held tog, purl.
Rnd 2 With D, knit.
Rnd 3 With B and D held tog, purl.
Rnd 4 With B, knit.
Rnd 5 With B and C held tog, purl.
Rnd 6 With C, knit.
Rnd 7 With A and C held tog, purl.
Rnd 8 With C, knit.
Rnd 9 With C and E held tog, purl.
Rnd 10 With E, knit.
Rnd 11 With B and E held tog, purl.
With B, bind off knitwise.

FINISHING
Weave in ends on the WS.❖

Chart A

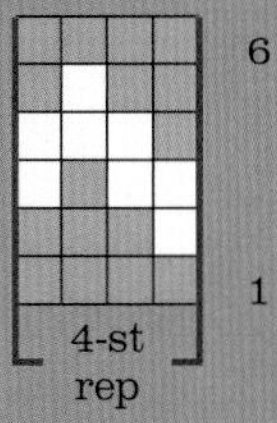

6

1

4-st
rep

Chart B

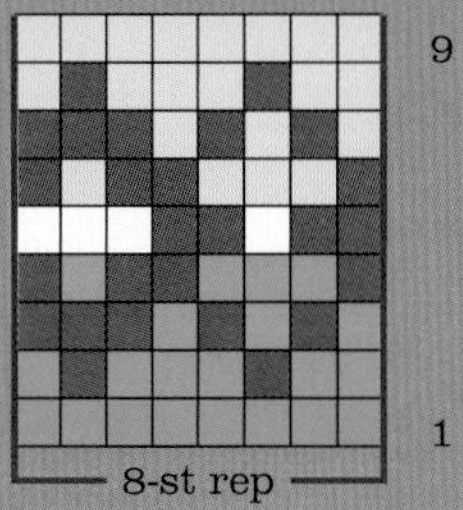

9

1

8-st rep

Chart C

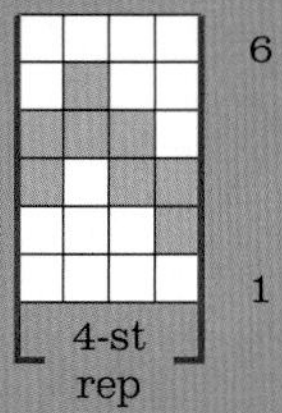

6

1

4-st
rep

Color Key

☐ A

■ B

☐ C

☐ D

☐ E

doubled-up

Keep it sweet and simple when you knit this cowl using three colors
in double-stranded tweed effect seed stitch.
Enhance your look with a decorator's tassel at the split-front neck.

■■□□

WHAT YOU NEED
Yarn
Mongolian Cashmere 4-Ply **by Jade
Sapphire, 2oz/55g hanks, each approx
200yd/183m (cashmere)** ④
• **1 hank each in #123 you say tomato (A),**
#119 mangrove (B), and #30 la nuit (C)

Needles
• **One size 7(4.5mm) circular needle,**
16"/40cm long or size to obtain gauge

Notions
• **Stitch marker**
• **Tapestry needle**

TASSEL COWL
Knit as a straight tube, this cowl creates
interest via color blending. Two colors
create tones and a third is added for depth.
The piece is finished with a hem of solid
color and then detailed with a tassel. Made
with cashmere, it's eye-popping luxury.

FINISHED MEASUREMENTS
Neck circumference 22"/56cm
Height 11½"/29cm

GAUGE
16 sts and 30 rnds = 4"/10cm over seed st
pat using 2 strands of yarn held tog and
size 7(4.5mm) needle.
Take time to check gauge.

SEED STITCH
(over an even number of sts and with 2
strands of yarn held tog)
Rnd (row) 1 *K1, p1; rep from * around (to
end).
Rnd (row) 2 K the purl and p the knit sts.
Rep rnd (row) 2 for seed st.

COWL
With 1 strand of A & B held tog, cast on 88
sts. Join to work in rnds, taking care not
to twist sts, and pm to mark beg of rnd.
Work in rnds of seed st with A & B held
tog for 3"/7.5cm. Cut B. Join C.
Work in seed st with A and C held tog
for 3"/7.5cm more. Cut A.
Join B. Work in seed st with B & C held
tog for 4½"/11.5cm more. Cut B and C.

Beg Split-Front
Join 2 strands of A and working back and
forth in rows, work in seed st for 1"/2.5cm
more. Bind off in pat.

FINISHING
Weave in ends on the WS.

Tassel
Cut a piece of cardboard to measure
5"/12.5cm. Wind colors A, B, and C approx
40 times around the cardboard. With
tapestry needle, thread several strands of
A and B through the top segment of the
loops. Fasten to the split opening of the
neck and fasten with a knot securely at the
base of this hanging loop. Cut yarn at the
opposite end of the cardboard to free the
tassel. Then, wind several strands around
the tassel at 1"/2.5cm from the top.
Trim the tassel ends.✤

a tale of two cowls

Create a modern take on tweed by alternating contrasting colors in this cowl pair. Seed stitch and a ruffling effect from three rows of bells offer fun pattern variations.

a tale of two cowls

■■■□

WHAT YOU NEED

Yarn

Zara Plus **by Filatura di Crosa/ Tahki·Stacy Charles, 1¾oz/50g balls, each approx 77yd/70m (wool)** 🔲
- **2 balls each in #08 dark blue (C) and #1973 medium blue (D)**
- **3 balls in #08 navy blue (A)**
- **4 balls in #1472 bright light blue (B)**

Needles

Long Cowl
- **One size 8 (5.5mm) circular needle, 29"/74cm long** or size to obtain gauge

Short Cowl
- **One size 8 (5mm) circular needle, 24"/60cm long** or size to obtain gauge

Notions
- **Stitch marker**
- **Tapestry needle**

LONG COWL/SHORT COWL

Interesting designs can be created with only two colors. Using one dark and one light color along with two stitch patterns, these cowls offer an intriguing contrast. Layer them with the bell facing upward or wear them separately. For additional contrast, add a completely different third color in the smaller cowl.

FINISHED MEASUREMENTS

Long Cowl
- **Circumference** 34"/86cm
- **Height** 12"/30.5cm

Short Cowl
- **Circumference** 22"/56cm
- **Height** 8"/20.5cm

GAUGE

17 sts and 34 rnds = 4"/10cm over seed st using size 8 (5mm) needle.
Take time to check gauge.

LONG COWL

SEED STITCH

(over an even number of sts)
Rnd 1 *K1, p1; rep from * around.
Rnd 2 *P1, k1; rep from * around.
Rep these 2 rnds for seed st.

COWL

With A and B held tog, cast on 144 sts. Join to work in rnds, taking care not to twist sts, and pm to mark beg of rnd. For the rem of cowl, work with 1 strand of either A or B for each rnd.
**Rnd 1 With B, work rnd 1 of seed st.
Rnd 2 With A, work rnd 2 of seed st**.
Rnds 3–18 Rep rnds 1 and 2 eight times more.
Begin Bell Pattern
Rnd 1 With A, *p4, cast on 6 sts; rep from * around. Drop A and cont to work with B for the next 7 rnds.
Rnd 2 With B, *p3, k7; rep from * around.
Rnd 3 *P3, ssk, k3, k2tog; rep from * around.
Rnd 4 *P3, k5; rep from * around.
Rnd 5 *P3, ssk, k1, k2tog; rep from * around.
Rnd 6 *P3, k3; rep from * around.
Rnd 7 *P3, SK2P; rep from * around.
Rnd 8 Purl.
Rnd 9 With A, purl.
Cont in bell pat as foll:
Rep rnds 1–9 once.
Rep rnds 1–7 once.
This completes the bell pattern +.
Rep from ** to ** in striped seed st until piece measures 12"/30.5cm from beg. Then, with A and B held tog, bind off in seed st pat.

FINISHING

Weave in ends on the WS.

SHORT COWL

SEED STITCH

(over an even number of sts)
Rnd 1 *K1, p1; rep from * around.
Rnd 2 *P1, k1; rep from * around.
Rep these 2 rnds for seed st.

COWL

With C and D held tog, cast on 92 sts. Join to work in rnds, taking care not to twist sts, and pm to mark beg of rnd. For the rem of cowl, work with 1 strand of either C or D for each rnd.
**Rnd 1 With D, work rnd 1 of seed st.
Rnd 2 With C, work rnd 2 of seed st**.
Rnds 3–10 Rep rnds 1 and 2 four times more.
Begin Bell Pattern
Work same as long cowl, rep rnds 1–9 twice then rnds 1–7 once, ending at +. Then rep from ** to ** in striped seed st until piece measures 8"/20.5cm from beg. Then, with C and D held tog, bind off in seed st pat.

FINISHING

Weave in ends on the WS.❖

ice rink princess

Be sure to pack this hood for your next trip to the rink
and watch your twirls, spins, and double axels earn perfect scores.

ice rink princess

■■■□

WHAT YOU NEED

Yarn

Beach Avenue Worsted **by North Light Fibers, 4oz/113g skeins, each approx 135yd/123m (alpaca/wool)** (4)
• **3 skeins in robin's egg**

Needles
• **One size 7 (4.5mm) circular needle, 24"/60cm long** or size to obtain gauge
• **Extra size 7 (4.5mm) needle for 3-needle bind-off**

Notions
• **Stitch marker**
• **Tapestry needle**
• **Pompom maker for 1½"/4cm pompoms**

LACE HOOD

The openwork slip stitch of this design creates a modern lace that is airy and light. As a bonus, the stitch works well either in the round or back and forth. Because it works up quickly, this lace hood is perfect as a speedy, last-minute knitting project for gift-giving.

FINISHED MEASUREMENTS

Width (at neck) 24"/61cm
Depth 18½"/46cm

GAUGE

16 sts and 20 rnds = 4"/10cm over openwork pattern stitch using size 7 (4.5mm) needle.
Take time to check gauge.

SEED STITCH RIB

(worked in rnds over an even number of sts)
Rnd 1 *K1, p1; rep from * around.
Rnd 2 Knit.
Rep rnds 1 and 2 for seed st rib.

OPENWORK PATTERN STITCH

(worked in rnds over a multiple of 4 sts)
Rnd 1 Knit.
Rnd 2 *K4, yo; rep from * to end.
Rnd 3 *Yo, sl 1, k3, pass the sl st over the k3 and drop the previous yo; rep from * around.
Rnd 4 Knit.
Rep rnds 1–4 for openwork pat st.

COWL

Cast on 96 sts and join to work in rnds, taking care not to twist sts on needle, and pm to mark beg of rnd.
Work 6 rnds in seed st rib.
Work openwork pattern stitch pat until there are a total of 11 reps and piece measures approx 8½"/21.5cm from beg, end with pat rnd 4.

Beg Hood

Note At this point, openwork pat st will be worked back and forth in rows for face opening as foll:
Row 1 (RS) Knit.
Row 2 (WS) *P4, yo; rep from * to the last 4 sts, end p4.
Row 3 K4, *drop the previous yo, then yo, sl 1, k3, pass the sl st over the k3; rep from * to the last 5 sts, drop the previous yo, then yo, sl 1, k1, psso, end k2.
Row 4 Purl.
Rep these 4 rows fourteen times more or for approx 10"/25.5cm.

FINISHING

Divide sts evenly between two needles and join the top of hood using the 3-needle bind-off method (see page 141).
Block finished piece lightly.
Make 3 pompoms and attach securely to the top corner of the hood.
Weave in ends on the WS.❖

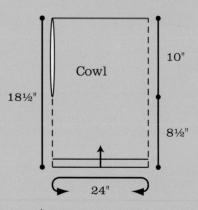

10"

Cowl

18½"

8½"

24"

↑ = Direction of work

— = Indicates 3-Needle Bind-Off

scrunch time

Simplify your morning routine with an easy neck cowl
to grab and pull on as you're heading out the door.

scrunch time

■■□□

WHAT YOU NEED
Yarn
Elements **by Berroco, 1¾oz/50g skeins, each approx 153yd/141m (wool/nylon)** (**4**)
• **2 skeins in #4937 bismuth**

Needles
• **One size 7 (4.5mm) circular needle, 16"/40cm long** or size to obtain gauge

Notions
• **Stitch marker**
• **Tapestry needle**
• **Two 2¾"/7cm length kilt pins**

SCRUNCHY COWL
Having my neck covered in cold weather makes me feel secure and cozy. Unlike a classic, straight-tube cowl, this design is tapered at the top with ribbing so that it warmly hugs the neck. Interest and asymmetry are created by adding kilt pins that are woven into picot verticals.

FINISHED MEASUREMENTS
Circumference 21"/53cm
Height 11"/28cm

GAUGE
23 sts and 28 rnds = 4"/10cm over pat st using size 7 (4.5mm) needle.
Take time to check gauge.

GARTER STITCH
(worked in rnds over any number of sts)
*Knit 1 rnd, purl 1 rnd; rep from * for garter st worked in rnds.

PATTERN STITCH
(worked in rnds over an even number of sts)
Rnd 1 Knit.
Rnd 2 P2tog around.
Rnd 3 Kfb in each st around.
Rnd 4 Knit.
Rep these 4 rnds for pat st worked in rnds.

K2, P2 RIB
(worked in rnds over a multiple of 4 sts)
Rnd 1 *K2, p2; rep from * around.
Rep rnd 1 for k2, p2 rib.

COWL
Beg at the lower edge, cast on 120 sts. Join to work in rnds, taking care not to twist sts, and pm to mark beg of rnd.
Rnds 1–4 Work even in garter st.
Eyelet rnd 5 K2, yo, k2tog, k to last 4 sts, k2tog, yo, k2.
Rnds 6–9 Work rnds 1–4 of pat st.
Rep rnds 5–9 for fourteen times more.

RIBBED TRIM
Dec rnd 1 [K8, k2tog] 12 times—108 sts.
Next rnd *K2, p2; rep from * around.
Cont in k2, p2 rib for 11 rnds more. Bind off in rib.

FINISHING
Weave in ends on the WS. To gather the cowl along the eyelet openings, start at the lower edge of the cowl and weave the first kilt pin up through one set of eyelet holes. Then, weave the other kilt pin down through a nearby set of eyelet holes to the lower edge of the cowl (see picture for reference).✤

grand   slam

Create a play on the classic tennis sweater!
Cables, ribs, and 3-color striping make for bold moves in this dickey-inspired cowl.

grand slam

■■■□

WHAT YOU NEED

Yarn
Cotton DK **by Debbie Bliss/KFI,**
1¾oz/50g balls, each approx
92yd/84m (cotton) ⬛
- **3 balls in #01 white (A)**
- **1 ball each in #18 navy (B) and**
#47 red (C)

Needles
- **One each size 5 (3.75mm) circular
needles, 16"/40cm, 24"/60cm, and
32"/80cm long** or size to obtain gauge

Notions
- **6 stitch markers**
- **Cable needle (cn)**
- **Tapestry needle**

SPORTY COWL DICKEY

A classic white tennis sweater came to
mind when designing this cowl dickey.
Nothing is snappier or sportier than
the bold combination of red, white, and
blue. To support your favorite sports
team or school, change up the colors!
Just remember to cold-water wash and
lay flat when cleaning.

FINISHED MEASUREMENTS

Circumference (At lower edge)
35"/89cm
**Circumference (At neck edge, slightly
stretched)** 22"/56cm
Height (with collar folded) 9"/23cm

GAUGE

22 and 26 rnds = 4"/10cm over k2, p2
rib, slightly stretched, using size 5
(3.75mm) needle.
Take time to check gauge.

K2, P2 RIB

(worked in rnds over a multiple of 4 sts)
Rnd 1 *K2, p2; rep from * around.
Rep rnd 1 for k2, p2 rib.

STITCH GLOSSARY

4-st RC Sl 2 sts to cn and hold to back,
k2, k2 from cn.
4-st LC Sl 2 sts to cn and hold to
front, k2, k2 from cn.

COWL

Beg at the top edge, with shortest
circular needle and A, cast on 112 sts.
Join to work in rnds, taking care not
to twist sts, and pm to mark beg of
rnd. Work in rnds of k2, p2 rib for
10"/25.5cm.
Note When working increases for
the neck edge of the cowl, change to
longer circular needle when there are
too many sts to fit comfortably on the
working needle.

Begin the Stripe Section
Set-up rnd 1 With A, k1, pm, k25
(for back), pm, k1, pm, k42 (for right
front), pm, k1, pm, k42 (for left front).

Inc rnd 2 With A, k1, sl marker, M1,
*k to next marker, M1, sl marker, k1,
sl marker, M1; rep from * once more,
k to next marker, M1, sl marker—6
sts inc'd and 118 sts.
Rnd 3 With B, knit around, slipping
markers.
Inc rnd 4 With B, rep inc rnd 2—124 sts.
Rnds 5 and 6 With A, rep rnds 3 and
4—130 sts.
Rnds 7–12 With C, rep rnds 3 and 4
three times more—148 sts.
Rnds 13 and 14 With A, rep rnds 3
and 4—154 sts.
Rnds 15 and 16 With B, rep rnds 3
and 4—160 sts.
Cut colors B and C and cont with A
only as foll:
Rnds 17 and 18 Rep rnds 3 and
4—166 sts.
Rnd 19 K1, sl marker, *p2, k4*; rep
between *s to 1 st before next marker,
p1, sl marker, k1, sl marker, rep
between *s to next marker, sl marker,
k1, sl marker, then **k4, p2; rep from
** to end.
Inc rnd 20 K1, sl marker, M1, *work
in rib to next marker, M1, sl marker,
k1, sl marker, M1; rep from * once
more, work in rib to next marker, M1,
sl marker—6 sts inc'd and 172 sts.
Rnd 21 Work in rib as established
with the inc'd sts in the rib pat.
Inc rnd 22 Rep inc rnd 20—178 sts.
Cable rnd 23 K1, sl marker, k2, *p2,
4-st RC*; rep between *s to 3 sts before
next marker, p2, k1, sl marker, k1,
sl marker, k2, rep between *s to 2 sts
before next marker, p2, sl marker, k1,
sl marker, **p2, 4-st LC**; rep between
**s to last 2 sts, k2, sl marker.
Inc rnd 24 Rep inc rnd 20—184 sts.
Rnd 25 Rep rnd 21.
Inc rnd 26 Rep inc rnd 20—190 sts.
Bind off in rib pat.

FINISHING

Weave in ends on the WS.❖

modern girl

Update your basic black or neutral wardrobe with this modern art cowl.
Short rows and color wedge flounces showcase a bold design.

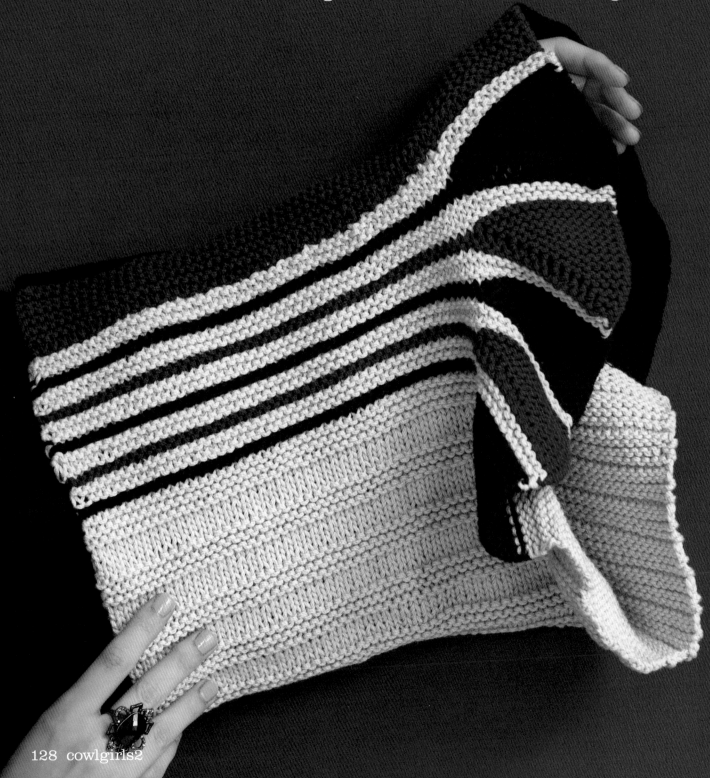

modern girl

■■■□

WHAT YOU NEED

Yarn
Weekend **by Berroco, 3½oz/100g hanks,
each approx 205yd/189m (acrylic/cotton)**[4]
• **1 hank each in #5903 oats (A), #5934
pitch black (B), and #5944 starry night (C)**

Needles
• **One size 6 (4mm) circular needle,
24"/60cm long** or size to obtain gauge

Notions
• **3 stitch markers**
• **Tapestry needle**

SHORT ROW COWL

This cowl is asymmetric in both form and
color placement, so pick three of your
favorite colors and go! If you love short
rows or have been eager to try them, this
pattern is just right. Note that because of
cotton's tendency to knot at the turn, the
short rows here do not involve wrapping
the end stitch.

FINISHED MEASUREMENTS

Circumference (at top edge) 21"/53cm
                (at bottom edge) 34"/86cm
Height 13"/33cm

GAUGE

20 sts and 32 rows = 4"/10cm over St st
using size 6 (4mm) needle.
Take time to check gauge.

NOTE

Do not wrap stitches when knitting short
rows.

GARTER STITCH

Working back and forth in rows, knit every
row.

COWL

With A, cast on 65 sts. Working back and
forth in rows, work as foll:
Rows 1–4 With A, knit.
Row 5 (RS) With B, knit.

Scallop
Short row 6 (WS) K15, turn.
Short row 7 and all odd short rows K
to end.
Short row 8 K14, turn.
Short row 10 K13, turn.
Short row 12 K12, turn.
Short row 14 K11, turn.
Short row 16 K10, turn.
Short row 18 K9, turn.
Short row 20 K8, turn.
Short row 22 K7, turn.
Short row 24 K6, turn.
Short row 26 K5, turn.
Short row 28 K4, turn.
Short row 30 K3, turn.
Short row 31 K to end.
Row 32 K to end on all 65 sts*.
Repeat rows 1–32 four times more using
A for rows 1–4 then alternating colors C,
B, C, and B for each resepective scallop. A
total of 5 scallops will be created after this
section is finished.

Back Wide Ridge Section
Rows 1–7 With A, knit.
Row 8 (WS) Purl.
Rows 9–11 Knit 1 row, purl 1 row, knit 1 row.
Rep rows 2–11 three times more.
Next 6 rows Knit.

Back Single Ridge Section
Row 1 (WS) With A, purl.

Rows 2–4 Knit.
Rows 5–7 Purl.
Rep rows 2–7 seven times more.
Next 3 rows Knit.
Next 2 rows Purl. The last row is worked
as a RS row. Cut A.

Flounce
Row 1 (WS) With B, purl.
Rows 2–4 Knit.
**Short row 5 (WS) K20, turn.
Short row 6 and all even short rows K
to end.
Short row 7 K19, turn.
Short row 9 K18, turn.
Short row 11 K17, turn.
Short row 13 K16, turn.
Short row 15 K15, turn.
Short row 17 K14, turn.
Short row 19 K13, turn.
Short row 21 K12, turn.
Short row 23 K11, turn.
Short row 25 K10, turn.
Short row 27 K9, turn.
Short row 29 K8, turn.
Short row 31 K7, turn.
Short row 33 K6, turn.
Short row 35 K5, turn.
Short row 37 K4, turn.
Short row 39 K3, turn.
Short row 40 K to end.**
Next 10 rows Knit.
Rep from ** to ** once more.
Next 15 rows Knit. Cut B.

Final Garter Stripe
Row 1 (WS) With C, purl.
Next 15 rows With C, knit.
Bind off knitwise with C.

FINISHING

Block piece lightly with steam to
measurements, being careful not to press
piece. Sew the bind-off edge to the cast-on
edge using tapestry needle and mattress st
worked from the RS. Weave in ends on the
WS.✣

split decision

Sit up and take notice! This structured cowl gently hugs the neck
while flaring out at the lower edge for a collar effect.

split decision

■■■□

WHAT YOU NEED

Yarn
Chunky **by Malabrigo, 3½oz/100g skeins, each approx 104yd/95m (wool)** ▣
- **1 skein in #CH193 jacinto (A)**
- **1 skein in #CH192 periwinkle (B)**

Needles
- **Two size 10½ (6.5mm) circular needles, each 20"/50 cm long** or size to obtain gauge

Notions
- **3 stitch markers**
- **Tapestry needle**

TWO-TONED COWL

Pick your favorite color in two tones for twice the fun! Knit in two halves, this cowl features a ribbed, split collar that connects with an overlapped purl stitch. The checked slip-stitch pattern highlights two colors of soft, chunky yarn.

FINISHED MEASUREMENTS

Circumference 19½"/49.5cm
Height (above collar) 7"/18cm
 (with collar) 9½"/24cm

GAUGE

13 sts and 26 rnds = 4"/10cm over slip stitch pattern using size 10½ (6.5mm) needles.
Take time to check gauge.

NOTE

This cowl is worked by starting with the split collar which is knit in two pieces (one in each color) then joined at the neck edge to work the slip-stitch pattern in rnds.

K1, P1 RIB

(worked in rows or rnds over an even number of sts)
Row (rnd) 1 (RS) *K1, p1; rep from * to end (around).
Rep row (rnd) 1 for k1, p1 rib.

SLIP-STITCH PATTERN

(worked in rnds over a multiple of 4 sts)
Rnd 1 With A, knit.
Rnd 2 With B, *sl 1 purlwise wyib, k3; rep from * around.
Rnds 3 and 4 Rep rnd 2.

Rnd 5 With B, knit.
Rnd 6 With A, *sl 1 purlwise wyib, k3; rep from * around.
Rnds 7 and 8 Rep rnd 6.
Rep these 8 rnds for slip-stitch pattern.

COWL

Collar
COLOR A
With A, cast on 66 sts. Working back and forth in rows, work in k1, p1 rib for 9 rows.
Dec row (RS) [K2tog tbl] 33 times—33 sts.
Lay piece aside
COLOR B
With B and other needle, work same as for collar in color A.

Neck
Beg working in rnds and join the 2 collar pieces from the RS as foll:
Joining rnd With color A piece on first needle and using color A, sl the last st of this collar onto the color B needle and p these 2 sts tog, then cont with A, k to 1 st before the end of this needle and p this last st tog with 1 st on first needle. Join and pm to mark beg of rnd—64 sts.
Then, beg with rnd 1, cont in slip-stitch pattern worked in rnds for a total of 5 reps of the 8-rnd pattern.
BEGIN 2-COLOR RIB
Rnd 1 *K1 with A, p1 with B; rep from * around.
Rnd 2 Rep rnd 1.
Bind off in the 2-color rib.

FINISHING
Weave in ends on the WS.❖

quality street

Azure hues work together in this extra-long tubular cowl. Wear it scrunched down to fill your open neckline or pulled up as a makeshift hood.

■■□□

WHAT YOU NEED
Yarn
Squishy **by Anzula, 1¾oz/50g hanks, each approx 385yd/352m (wool/cashmere/nylon)** ⟨**1**⟩
• **1 hank each in denim (A), paradise (B), seaside (C), elephant (D), and chiva (E)**

Needles
• **One size 2 (2.75mm) circular needle, 24"/60cm long** or size to obtain gauge

Notions
• **Stitch marker**
• **Tapestry needle**

TUBULAR COWL
"Yummy" sums up this luxurious, minimalist, color-blocked cowl. It's about as easy as it gets technically and the 40-inch length will start to fly as you pick up speed. Pick your five favorite colors and, as a bonus, use the leftover yarn for a coordinating hat!

FINISHED MEASUREMENTS
Circumference 26"/66 cm
Depth 40"/101.5cm

GAUGE
30 sts and 40 rnds = 4"/10cm over St st using size 2 (2.75mm) needle.
Take time to check gauge.

SEED STITCH
(over an odd number of sts)
Rnd 1 K1, *p1, k1; rep from * around.
Rnd 2 P1, *k1, p1; rep from * around.
Rep rnds 1 and 2 for seed st.

STOCKINETTE STITCH
(worked in rnds over any number of sts)
Knit every rnd.

COWL
A Stripe
With A, cast on 195 sts. Join, taking care not to twist sts on needle, and pm to mark beg of rnd. Working in seed st, work even for 4"/10cm. Then, change to St st and cont with A in St st for 4"/10cm more. Cut A.
B Stripe
With B, work in St st for 8"/20.5cm more. Cut B.
C Stripe
With C, work in St st for 8"/20.5cm more. Cut C.
D Stripe
With D, work in St st for 8"/20.5cm more. Cut D.
E Stripe
With E, work in St st for 4"/10cm more. Then cont with E in seed st for 4"/10cm. Bind off in pat.

FINISHING
Weave in ends on the WS. Block lightly to measurements. ✣

changing it up: converting

Cowls and gaiters work up beautifully when knitted in the round (ITR). However, most stitch patterns are written for working back and forth (B&F) to create flat pieces. The patterns in this book are written for the specific structure, so no adjustments are needed, but if you have a favorite B&F stitch pattern that you want to work ITR, here is how you can convert it. It's easier than you might think.

Let's take the most basic stitch patterns to start: **stockinette and garter stitches**. To work stockinette stitch B&F, you just alternate knitting a row and purling a row. To achieve the same stitch pattern ITR, all you need to do is knit every row; in effect you have made the alternate row the opposite of what it was when it was worked B&F (i.e., the knits are now purls and the purls are now knit stitches). Written out it would look like this:

Stockinette stitch	**Worked B&F**		**Worked ITR**
	Row 1 Knit.	>>>>	**Row 1** Knit.
	Row 2 Purl.	>>>>	**Row 2** Knit.

Garter stitch is converted similarly: When worked B&F all you do is knit, but to achieve that same look ITR, you have to reverse the alternate row:

Garter stitch	**Worked B&F**		**Worked ITR**
	Row 1 Knit.	>>>>	**Row 1** Knit.
	Row 2 Knit.	>>>>	**Row 2** Purl.

That was easy, so let's try something a bit more challenging, like seed, or moss, stitch, which has both knits and purls in a row. In this case you just change each stitch in the alternate rows in the B&F version of the pattern to its opposite, while maintaining the same stitch multiple of the pattern in each row:

Seed stitch	**Worked B&F**		**Worked ITR**
(multiple of 2 sts)	**Row 1** K1, p1.	>>>>	**Row 1** K1, p1.
	Row 2 P1, k1.	>>>>	**Row 2** K1, p1.

OK, let's step it up a bit and try a cable pattern, which has more than two rows and a

from B&F to ITR

row where the cable twist occurs. How do you work a cable "backward"? It's really not as tricky as it sounds. Analyze the pattern you want to convert and decide which would be the hardest row to convert to its "opposite." For a cable pattern, that would be the row in which the cable is twisted. Make that the row you don't convert—**keep it intact as written in the B&F version**. If it is an odd row, keep all of the odd rows the same and convert just the even rows; if it is an even row, keep all the even rows the same and convert just the odd rows.

Cable and seed stitch pattern (over a multiple of 16 sts plus 8)

Worked B&F
Rows 1, 5 and 7 (RS) [K1, p1] 4 times, *p1, k6, p1, [p1, k1] 4 times; rep from * to end.
Rows 2, 4 and 6 *[P1, k1] 4 times, k1, p6, k1; rep from *, end [k1, p1] 4 times.
Row 3 [K1, p1] 4 times, *p1, 6-st RC, p1, [p1, k1] 4 times; rep from * to end.
Row 8 Rep row 2.

Worked ITR
Rows 1, 5 and 7 (RS) [K1, p1] 4 times, *p1, k6, p1, [p1, k1] 4 times; rep from * to end. (Stays the same.)
Rows 2, 4, 6 and 8 *[K1, p1] 4 times, p1, k6, p1; rep from *, end [p1, k1] 4 times. (Change these rows.)
Row 3 [K1, p1] 4 times, *p1, 6-st RC, p1, [p1, k1] 4 times; rep from * to end. (Stays the same.)

Row 3 above in the B&F version is where the cable twist (6-st RC) occurs, so keep that one, as well as every **odd row**, as is. In turn, rewrite every **even row** to be the opposite—change the knit stitches into purl stitches and the purl stitches into knit stitches.

Just about every pattern, even lace patterns, can be converted to work ITR, although some may be tougher to figure out than others. Convert lace patterns in the same way: Figure which row in the pattern would be hardest to write the inverse of and make that the one you leave untouched. If it's an odd row, leave all other odd rows untouched. If it's an even row, leave those untouched and change the odd rows. Finally, as they say, "The proof is in the pudding," and in knitting, the "pudding" is a test swatch!

things to know

abbreviations

approx	approximately
beg	begin(ning)
CC	contrasting color
ch	chain
cm	centimeter(s)
cn	cable needle
cont	continu(e)(ing)
dec	decreas(e)(ing)
dpn(s)	double-pointed needle(s)
foll	follow(s)(ing)
g	gram(s)
inc	increas(e)(ing)
itr	in-the-round
k	knit
kfb	knit into front and back of stitch
k2tog	knit 2 stitches together
LH	left-hand
lp(s)	loop(s)
m	meter(s)
MB	make bobble
MC	main color
mm	millimeter(s)
M1	make one: with needle tip, lift strand between last stitch knit (purled) and the next stitch on the LH needle and knit (purl) into back of it
oz	ounce(s)
p	purl
pat(s)	pattern(s)
pm	place marker
psso	pass slip stitch(es) over
p2tog	purl 2 stitches together
rem	remain(s)(ing)
rep	repeat
RH	right-hand
rnd(s)	round(s)
RS	right side(s)
SKP	slip 1, knit 1, pass slip stitch over
SK2P	slip 1, knit 2 together, pass slip stitch over the knit 2 together
sl	slip
sl st	slip stitch
ssk	slip, slip, knit
ssp	slip, slip, purl
sssk	slip, slip, slip, knit
st(s)	stitch(es)
St st	stockinette stitch
S2KP	slip 2 stitches together, knit 1, pass 2 slip stitches over knit 1
tbl	through back loop(s)
tog	together
WS	wrong side(s)
wyib	with yarn in back
wyif	with yarn in front
yd	yard(s)
yo	yarn over needle
*****	repeat directions following * as many times as indicated
[ ]	repeat directions inside brackets as many times as indicated

skill levels

■□□□
beginner
Ideal first project.

■■□□
easy
Basic stitches, minimal shaping, and simple finishing.

■■■□
intermediate
For knitters with some experience. More intricate stitches, shaping, and finishing.

■■■■
experienced
For knitters able to work patterns with complicated shaping and finishing.

gauge

Make a test swatch at least 4"/10cm square. If the number of stitches and rows does not correspond to the gauge given, you must change the needle size. An easy rule to follow is: To get fewer stitches to the inch/cm, use a larger needle; to get more stitches to the inch/cm, use a smaller needle. Continue to try different needle sizes until you get the same number of stitches in the gauge.

knitting needles

US.	METRIC
0	2mm
1	2.25mm
2	2.75mm
3	3.25mm
4	3.5mm
5	3.75mm
6	4mm
7	4.5mm
8	5mm
9	5.5mm
10	6mm
10½	6.5mm
11	8mm
13	9mm
15	10mm
17	12.75mm
19	15mm
35	19mm

techniques

cable cast-on

1. Make a slipknot on the left needle. Insert the right needle knitwise into the stitch on the left needle. Wrap the yarn around the right needle as if to knit.

2. Draw the yarn through the first stitch to make a new stitch, but do not drop the stitch from the left needle.

3. Slip the new stitch to the left needle as shown.

4. *Insert the right needle between the two stitches on the left needle.

5. Wrap the yarn around the right needle as if to knit and pull the yarn through to make a new stitch.

6. Place the new stitch on the left needle as shown. Repeat from the *, always inserting the right needle in between the last two stitches on the left needle.

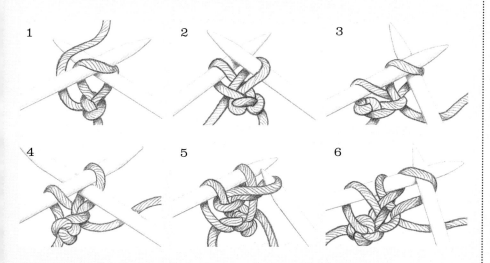

yarn overs
between two knit stitches

between two purl stitches

Bring the yarn from the back of the work to the front between the two needles. Knit the next stitch, bringing the yarn to the back over the right-hand needle, as shown.

Leave the yarn at the front of the work. Bring the yarn to the back over the right-hand needle and to the front again, as shown. Purl the next stitch.

3-needle bind-off

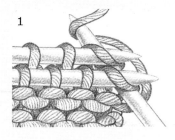

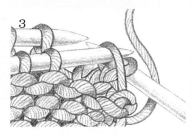

1. With the right side of the two pieces facing each other, and the needles parallel, insert a third needle knitwise into the first stitch of each needle. Wrap the yarn around the needle as if to knit.

2. Knit these two stitches together and slip them off the needles. *Knit the next two stitches together in the same way as shown.

3. Slip the first stitch on the third needle over the second stitch and off the needle. Repeat from the * in step 2 across the row until all the stitches are bound off.

techniques

beaded knitting

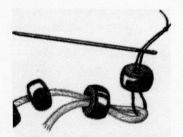

To add beads in stockinette stitch on right-side rows, beads are placed without the purl stitches on either side. The bead will lie directly in front of the stitch. Work the stitch firmly so that the bead won't fall to the back of the work.

To add beads in stockinette stitch on right-side rows, beads are placed without the purl stitches on either side. The bead will lie directly in front of the stitch. Work the stitch firmly so that the bead won't fall to the back of the work.

From the right side:
Work to the stitch to be beaded, then slip the bead up in back of the work. Insert needle as if to knit; wrap yarn around it. Push bead to front through the stitch on the left needle; complete the stitch.

picking up stitches along horizontal edge

1. Insert the knitting needle into the center of the first stitch in the row below the bound-off edge. Wrap the yarn knitwise around the needle.

2. Draw the yarn through. You have picked up one stitch. Continue to pick up one stitch in each stitch along the bound-off edge.

picking up stitches along vertical edge

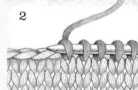

1. Insert the knitting needle into the corner stitch of the first row, one stitch in from the side edge. Wrap the yarn around the needle knitwise.

2. Draw the yarn through. You have picked up one stitch. Continue to pick up stitches along the edge. Occasionally skip one row to keep the edge from flaring.

wrap and turn

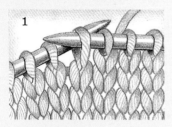
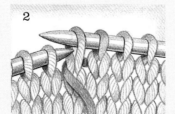
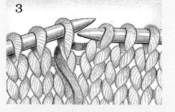

1. To prevent holes in the piece and create a smooth transition, wrap a knit stitch as follows: With the yarn in back, slip the next stitch purlwise.

2. Move the yarn between the needle to the front of the work.

3. Slip the same stitch back to the left needle. Turn the

work, bringing the yarn to the purl side between the needles. One stitch is wrapped.

4. When you have completed all the short rows, you must hide the wraps. Work to just before the wrapped stitch. Insert the right needles under the wrap and knitwise into the wrapped stitch. Knit them together.

weaving other stitches

1

2

1. If you have left a long tail from your cast-on row, you can use this strand to begin sewing. To make a neat join at the lower edge with no gap, use the technique shown here. Thread the strand into a yarn needle. With the right sides of both pieces facing you, insert the yarn needle from back to front into the corner stitch of the piece without the tail. Making a figure eight with the yarn, insert the needle from back to front into the stitch with the cast-on tail. Tighten to close the gap.

2. To make an invisible side seam in a garment worked in stockinette stitch, insert the yarn needle under the horizontal bar between the first and second stitches. Insert the needle into the corresponding bar on the other piece. Pull the yarn gently until the sides meet. Continue alternating from side to side.

resources

Anzula
740 H Street
Fresno, CA 93721
www.anzula.com

Berroco
1 Tupperware Drive, Suite 4
N. Smithfield, RI 02896-6815
www.berroco.com

Blue Sky Alpacas
P.O. Box 88
Cedar, MN 55011
www.blueskyalpacas.com

Cascade Yarns
1224 Andover Park East
Tukwila, WA 98188
www.cascadeyarns.com

Classic Elite Yarns
16 Esquire Road, Unit 2
North Billerica, MA 01862-2500
www.classiceliteyarns.com

Debbie Bliss
Distributed by KFI
315 Bayview Avenue
Amityville, NY 11701
www.debbieblissonline.com

Filatura di Crosa
Distributed by Tahki Stacy
Charles, Inc.
774 Haunted Lane
Bensalem, PA 19020
www.tahkistacycharles.com

**Imperial Yarn Div
of Farm to Finery**
58150 Highway 197
Tygh Valley, OR 97063
www.imperialyarn.com

Jade Sapphire Exotic Fibres
146 Germonds Road
West Nyack, NY 10994
www.jadesapphire.com

Knit One, Crochet Too, Inc.
91 Tandberg Trail, Unit 6
Windham, ME 04062
www.knitonecrochettoo.com

Louisa Harding Yarns
www.louisaharding.co.uk

Madelinetosh
3430 Alameda Street
Suite 112
Ft. Worth, TX 76126
www.madelinetosh.com

Malabrigo
www.malabrigo.com

Misti Alpaca, Inc. USA
P.O. Box 2532
Glen Ellyn, IL 60138
www.mistialpaca.com

North Light Fibers
P.O. Box 1382
129 Spring Street
Block Island, RI 02807
www.northlightfibers.com

Quince & Co.
www.quinceandco.com

Rowan Yarns
Green Lane Mill
Holmfirth
West Yorkshire
England
HD9 2DX
www.knitrowan.com

Swan's Island
231 Atlantic Highway
(US Route 1)
Northport, ME 04849
www.swansislandcompany.com

Trendsetter Yarns
16745 Saticoy Street, #101
Van Nuys, CA 91406
www.trendsetteryarns.com

index